AMERICA'S
YOUNGEST
AMBASSADOR

THE COLD WAR STORY OF SAMANTHA SMITH'S LASTING MESSAGE OF PEACE

LENA NELSON

Down East Books
CAMDEN, MAINE

Down East Books

Published by Down East Books
An imprint of Globe Pequot, the trade division of
The Rowman & Littlefield Publishing Group, Inc.
4501 Forbes Blvd., Ste. 200
Lanham, MD 20706
www.rowman.com
www.downeastbooks.com

Distributed by NATIONAL BOOK NETWORK

Library of Congress Cataloging-in-Publication Data
Names: Nelson, Lena, 1975– author.
Title: America's youngest ambassador: the Cold War story of Samantha Smith's lasting message of peace / Lena Nelson.
Other titles: Cold War story of Samantha Smith's lasting message of peace
Description: Lanham, MD : Derrydale Press, [2023] | Includes bibliographical references.
Identifiers: LCCN 2022042063 (print) | LCCN 2022042064 (ebook) | ISBN 9781684750207 (cloth) | ISBN 9781684750214 (epub)
Subjects: LCSH: Smith, Samantha, 1972–1985—Influence. | Smith, Samantha, 1972–1985—Correspondence. | United States—Relations—Soviet Union. | Soviet Union—Relations—United States. | Andropov, I͡U. V. (I͡Uriĭ Vladimirovich), 1914–1984—Correspondence. | Cold War. | Children—United States—Biography. | Maine—Biography. | Nelson, Lena, 1975- —Childhood and youth. | Arkhangelʹsk (Russia)—Biography.
Classification: LCC CT275.S5525 N45 2023 (print) | LCC CT275.S5525 (ebook) | DDC 973.927/0924 [B]—dc23/eng/20220907
LC record available at https://lccn.loc.gov/2022042063
LC ebook record available at https://lccn.loc.gov/2022042064

∞™ The paper used in this publication meets the minimum requirements of American National Standard for Information Sciences—Permanence of Paper for Printed Library Materials, ANSI/NISO Z39.48-1992.

For my children, Kenny and Nikki—
always remember, one person can make a difference.

And for Jane.

CONTENTS

Prologue ix

PART I: LETTER. 1
  1 Mourning Ribbons. 3
  2 *Who* Wants War?. 11
  3 "Why Don't *You?*" 17
  4 "My Age Has Nothing to Do with It". 23
  5 Live on National TV. 31
  6 Janie 35
  7 "Are You Tired of Answering All These Questions?" 41
  8 Mr. Mom. 45
  9 04351 to 163001 49
10 Four Minutes to Midnight. 57
11 "She Needs to See the Answers for Herself". 63

PART II: JOURNEY **69**
12 Northern Summer 71
13 On Our Way. 75
14 The Lemony Scent of Cypress 83
15 "The Warriors of the Invisible Front" 93
16 "I Love You, Artek!" 99
17 "So Do the Russians Want War?" 115
18 "Samantha Put the Soviets in Color" 125

v

PART III: WELCOME HOME! **135**

19 Welcome Home, Samantha! 137

20 "Look Around and See Only Friends". 143

21 Samantha Smith Goes to Washington. 151

22 *Lime Street* 161

23 Bar Harbor 1808 167

24 "A Great Ambassador" 173

25 SAME 181

Epilogue 189

Acknowledgments 193

References 197

About the Author 209

We love and lose in China,
we weep on England's moors,
and laugh and moan in Guinea,
and thrive on Spanish shores.

We seek success in Finland,
are born and die in Maine.
In minor ways we differ,
in major we're the same.

I note the obvious differences
between each sort and type,
but we are more alike, my friends,
than we are unalike.

We are more alike, my friends,
than we are unalike.

—FROM "HUMAN FAMILY,"
A POEM BY MAYA ANGELOU

PROLOGUE

On August 28, 1985, the pews at St. Mary's Church in Augusta, Maine, were filling up quickly. When a black limousine pulled up to its doors and a tall man in his thirties stepped out, reporters closed ranks around him on the church steps. The man's name was Vladimir Kulagin, and he was the first secretary for cultural affairs at the Soviet embassy in Washington, DC. Kulagin had obtained a special clearance from the State Department to travel to Kennebec County, one of the ten Maine counties that were off limits to Soviet citizens in the summer of 1985. This concession, a rare pause in the Soviet-American conflict, was granted so that Kulagin could attend a memorial service for a thirteen-year-old American schoolgirl, Samantha Smith, and her father, Arthur, who had been killed in a plane crash near Auburn, Maine, just three days earlier.

Kulagin paused and turned to the microphones. "She was like a ray of sunshine with her smile, her frankness, openness, her friendship. . . . We saw her, this small girl, as a big, great ambassador. You know? And . . . millions of Soviet people judged the American people by her."

Two days earlier, on the evening of August 26, 1985, on the other side of the world, I was packing my schoolbag, wondering what the fourth grade would be like. Every school year in the Soviet Union started on the same day—September 1, my birthday. This one would be my tenth. I largely ignored the cacophony of the evening news broadcast on our black-and-white TV until it was suddenly interrupted by the commentator's somber voice: "The terrible news has just crossed the ocean. Samantha Smith is no more." I turned to the TV and froze.

I'd never met Samantha Smith. The little girl from the tiny Maine town of Manchester lived too far away from my Soviet hometown of

Arkhangelsk. She only smiled at me from my TV screen and photographs in the newspapers as she and her family toured my country in the summer of 1983.

Yet, in that moment, when I heard that she and her father had died in a plane crash in Maine, the fragility of life became very real to me. I don't remember whether I lowered my school notebook into my bag or carried it to the couch where I sat for a while, stunned. Where had she been going, and where was she coming from? I imagined the crash, the plane falling from the sky. Did she know what was happening? Or maybe she had been asleep.

"Yesterday, when I went to my friend's house, she might have been packing her suitcase," I said to no one in particular. I found this rewind comforting, and so I retraced my own steps back in time—and imagined what yesterday might have been like for her, grasping at the moments to which I was not privy but which held her smiling, alive.

Twenty-one years later, on a waning afternoon in August 2006, I followed Jane Smith out of the Maine State Museum to the bronze statue of her only child. Lush birch trees filtered the weary rays of sunshine on the likeness of a little girl with shoulder-length hair and a toothy grin. The girl, dressed in a polo shirt, jeans, and tennis shoes, held a peace dove in her outstretched hands. A bear cub, a symbol of both Maine and Russia, sat at her feet.

"I used to buy those polo shirts at Sears," Jane said. "You know, sometimes in the winter, I think that she might be cold out here."

Technically, this is not my first attempt to record the remarkable story of Samantha Smith. On hearing the news of her tragic death, I wanted to do something to preserve her memory, so I started a collection of newspaper clippings about her from as many Soviet newspapers as I could locate. I glued my findings into school notebooks, and by the time I was twelve, my collection fit into seven of them. Then I got the brilliant idea of binding them into a book. I asked my mom whether she or any of her friends knew anything about bookbinding; on learning that they did not, I embarked on the project on my own.

Taking apart an old math textbook, I imitated its design. I used two large pieces of cardboard for the book covers and the book spine. I maneuvered my scissors to carefully cut the brown vinyl my mom had procured from her coworkers and folded it neatly over the covers. For several hours, I holed up in my family's only bathroom, using a washing machine as a workbench. Finally, my finished project—a thick brown scrapbook—was ready to be set under a stack of textbooks to dry flat. While not aesthetically pleasing, it was very functional and kept my entire collection together. Thirty-some years later, it still sits on my bookshelf: it was among the few items that I brought along in my suitcase when, in 1995, I moved to the United States after getting married.

I looked through that scrapbook again with my mother when she came to visit me in 2003, and we talked about my late grandmother, Baba Valia, who had been a great fan of Samantha Smith. I was seven when Baba Valia showed me the newspaper article with the letter Samantha had written to our Soviet leader, Yuri Andropov. She called her "Samantka," since Russian doesn't have a "th" sound. Baba Valia held the ten-year-old American in high esteem, reprimanding me with "Samantka wouldn't do that" if I misbehaved. She felt that Samantha Smith was an example worth following.

That evening, after my mom went to bed, I typed "Samantha Smith" into my online search engine. I was shocked to discover that a story that once had such wide news coverage on both sides of the ocean had no online presence. Except for a short mention on a US/Russian sister-city page of the Samantha Smith Foundation, started by Samantha's mother, Jane, after her daughter's death, there was nothing to be found about Samantha Smith. How could this be? How could she have been forgotten? "Someone should make a website about her," I thought to myself. But I had no idea how to make a website. So, instead, the next morning I wrote a letter. Very Samantha-like, I suppose. I used the contact info for the Samantha Smith Foundation and addressed the envelope to her mother, Jane Smith. I told her that her daughter was my childhood hero and thanked her for Samantha.

A couple weeks later, a trip to the mailbox revealed an envelope with a return address that read "J. Smith." I stood staring at it for a while. An answer I never expected to receive made me feel strangely connected to my childhood. I opened the envelope as I walked down the hill to my house. "Your story is very interesting to me," Jane wrote, "and helpful—to know what Samantha's 'adventure' meant to you." Jane asked me whether I knew that Portland, Maine, was a sister city with my hometown of Arkhangelsk. I don't know why she wrote back to me—good manners, I suppose—but I knew then that I would need to figure out how to make that website.

I had no idea that a letter I didn't expect to get an answer to would be the start of an adventure of my own. It took me two years to get started with web design, but in May 2005, when my family caught a flu bug and for two weeks asked only for snacks and water, I finally figured out how to use a website template, and www.SamanthaSmith.info went live. That summer I was planning to be on the East Coast, and so I contacted Jane again to ask whether it would be possible to meet her and shake her hand. "Yes," she replied, "let's meet at the statue in Augusta." In August of that year, along with my seven-year-old son and four-year-old daughter, my husband, and my mother, I stood looking up at a bronze statue of a smiling girl holding a dove in her hands. A few minutes later, I saw Jane. I recognized her by her walk, which I'd seen on TV when I was little. Fast, determined, she walked up the hill from the parking lot and came up to me with her hand outstretched. I stretched out mine.

Jane was remarkably friendly to a complete stranger. We chatted about the kids' interests; she commented on how my mother and I looked alike. "So do you and your daughter," replied my mom, pointing at the statue. We took a picture together. A month or so later, I told Jane about the website I had made. She loved it, it turned out. She had wanted to make one for years, she said, but hadn't known how.

As I watched the website traffic grow, emails from around the world began to arrive regularly—with tributes as well as scans of news clippings. Many of the senders were my contemporaries who had scrapbooks just like mine. Some offered help with translating articles, others with digitizing videos. As years passed, images from my site spread around the Internet, and then the American and Russian news agencies uploaded their own photographs of Samantha's trip. Long forgotten, they finally were back on display. In 2007, the US embassy in Russia included an article about Samantha on its history of Soviet-American relations page. Most rewarding, though, were the emails from schoolchildren who had questions about Samantha for their National History Day projects.

As I scoured the now-defunct Google newspaper archive late into the night, I kept asking myself why I was so determined to preserve this particular story now that the Cold War was over. It seemed to me back then that correcting the injustice of Samantha's story being forgotten was somehow important.

"History is fickle," a friend of mine, a former war correspondent, once said. "Out of it we pull the tiny kernels that touched us in a singular way; whatever we take the time to remember, will be remembered after us. The rest will be lost." The story of Samantha Smith touched me in that *singular* way; hence I will take the time to remember.

Samantha Reed Smith was born on June 29, 1972, in Houlton, Maine. I was born three years later in Arkhangelsk, a northern port city of the Soviet Union. I've never thought of us as "we." And yet we were two girls who lived on different sides of the ocean at a time when our two countries were each other's greatest enemies.

PART I

LETTER

In June 2014, Russia's Federal Archives marked the hundredth birthday of Yuri Andropov with an exhibition of declassified documents detailing the reticent Soviet leader's life. Among the transcripts of the Politburo meetings and the general secretary's correspondence with the heads of state was a letter from President Ronald Reagan congratulating him on his election to the post of chairman of the Presidium of the Supreme Soviet of the Union of Soviet Socialist Republics. Next to it was a letter penned on yellow note paper in a careful, childish scrawl. It was signed "Samantha Smith. P.S. Please write back."

1

MOURNING RIBBONS

NOVEMBER 1982, ARKHANGELSK, USSR

I was seven years old when Leonid Brezhnev died at 8:30 a.m. on November 10, 1982, at his dacha on the outskirts of Moscow. His death at the age of seventy-five, and with it the end of his eighteen-year rule, weren't reported until the next day, when all the Soviet radio stations played solemn music and the announcer's grave voice read the news at 10:00 a.m.

Thursday, November 11, started as just another school day. Our homeroom teacher, Nina Mikhailovna, taught all the first-grade subjects—from math to arts—in our third-floor classroom at Arkhangelsk School #21. A mother of three, she was a strict but kind lady in her early forties. Her short blond curls fell gracefully over her ears, and she had a beautiful smile—when she felt like smiling. Around midday that day, it took longer than usual to get going with instructions for the next task.

Nina Mikhailovna surveyed the class, and then, in a very formal voice, she said she had some *very sad* news. The general secretary of the Central Committee of the Communist Party of the Soviet Union, Leonid Il'ich Brezhnev, had died "a sudden death."

I was confused by the "sudden" part. The word in Russian literally meant that death had sneaked up on him. But how could this happen to someone so important? Wasn't someone supposed to know that he was sick and could die? The fact that he was gone and that I should be grieving didn't really register. Nina Mikhailovna's demeanor was somber, and

I could tell that she expected us to follow suit. Somewhat unprepared for the mood, I lowered my eyes to stare at my notebook.

"Find the portrait of Leonid Il'ich toward the back of your textbook," she instructed us. The rustle of pages spread across the classroom as we located the image.

In the textbook he looked younger than the man I frequently saw on the huge posters of Politburo members that my mom's coworkers carried during the October Revolution Day or International Worker's Day parades. The black-and-white portraits, nailed to long sticks, were handed to people in the parade on those government holidays. The tall men in fedora hats distributing them would ask jokingly, "Who wants to carry Gromyko? Ustinov anyone?"

I sensed a degree of contempt in their remarks, but at a young age I didn't quite understand all that it meant. Sometimes I saw those "men in the portraits" on my black-and-white TV—they used big words strung into very long sentences. I wondered how they could say so much and yet I understood so little.

Pravdist, the tiny bookstore on my street corner, which I checked regularly for postcards with drawings of bears and hedgehogs, also had a large portrait of Brezhnev on its wall. In all his portraits, Brezhnev reminded me of a big, silent bear, and I found his sagging mouth funny, a notion I didn't share with anyone, somehow sensing its inappropriateness.

Brezhnev in my textbook seemed to crack a slight smile. He was wearing a dark suit, his shoulders so large they disappeared past the margins of the frame. Four gold stars adorned the left side of his chest, and four round medals graced the right; he wore a small, red flag pin on his left lapel. "He must have been a real war hero to get so many awards," I concluded as I counted them.

"Get out your rulers," said Nina Mikhailovna. "Find your black pencils." I lifted the lid of my orange plastic pencil box to reveal a set of colored pencils. Locating the black one, I sat ready for the next set of instructions.

"In the lower right corner of the page you will make two diagonal lines—to form a black mourning ribbon—just like the black ribbons you will see everywhere today when you go home." I'd seen the mourning ribbons before at the houses of my friends who had lost a grandparent. A black silk ribbon stretching across the lower right corner of a photograph for some reason made me look at the image longer than usual, compelling me to imagine their loss.

With a piece of white chalk, Nina Mikhailovna made a large rectangle on the blackboard and then carefully marked the lower right corner with two diagonal lines. She stepped back to show us—the black of the board between the two white chalk lines did indeed look like a mourning ribbon.

It made no sense to me to use a ruler for art, but I feared that freehanding a ribbon on such a day was out of the question. Despite my best efforts at manipulating the ruler, my seven-year-old hands couldn't manage a perfect ribbon. When Nina Mikhailovna walked around to inspect our work, I casually rested the brown sleeve of my school dress to cover up the crookedness of my mourning ribbon.

"Now," Nina Mikhailovna said, back at the blackboard. Her eyes settled on slender Katia Kozlova, who sat across the aisle from me. Already the shortest girl in our class, Katia looked even smaller in her brown school dress and black apron. Her braids, crisscrossed at the back of her head, almost managed to control her unruly curls—just a tiny bit of the dandelion-like fuzz gathered around her bows. In class Katia was studious, but her sweet nature made her a cheerful companion at breaks. "Would you please read to us what it says, Katia," Nina Mikhailovna instructed. Katia nodded in response. "Everyone, follow along as Katia reads."

Katia started reading the four lines of text under the portrait. "Leonid Il'ich Brezhnev, the general secretary of the Central Committee of the Communist Party of the Soviet Union." Those big words had way too many syllables. Only two months into the first grade, I had a hard time navigating the lines. My finger followed aimlessly, my eyes unable to form words at Katia's speed.

I was grateful that Nina Mikhailovna hadn't asked me. Unlike Katia and some of my other classmates who read well before entering school, I was among those students whose parents, for one reason or another, felt that reading was learned in the classroom. I suspected Nina Mikhailovna realized that this was no occasion for sounding out syllables.

My finger hunted for white spaces where a pause might indicate Katia's location. At one point the pause seemed too long. "Did she trip on that big word? Or maybe this one?" My finger rested in the middle of line three. I snuck a glance at her. She was crying. Quiet sobs at first, followed by loud sniffling. Nina Mikhailovna seemed at a loss for words and willing to wait. Katia pulled a handkerchief out of her pocket and tried to continue, but sobs overpowered her again. "Why would anyone cry because they didn't know how to read a word?" I thought to myself. Suddenly it hit me: Katia knew how to read those words. She knew how to read all of them. She was sad that he had died.

I felt ashamed. I couldn't push a tear out even if I tried. I looked at Katia again. She wiped her nose. With some effort, she finished reading: "Chairman of the Presidium of the Supreme Soviet of the USSR." The four lines of text were his title. I scanned it again—for the first time realizing the scale of grief I was supposed to feel.

"Now look at the page on the right," said Nina Mikhailovna. On it five children in colorful folk costumes were walking hand in hand. "Leonid Il'ich stood for peace," Nina Mikhailovna said. "Katia, can you continue?" Katia composed herself and turned to read the text under the picture: "Children of many nationalities live on this blue planet we call Earth. They might have different skin color. They might speak different languages. But all of them wish for happiness and bright sunlit sky. Soviet children want to be friends with the children all over the world. And work for peace. Children of many lands, we all live with a dream of peace."

"Why am I not sad?" I asked myself over and over, but no answer came to me. I made a mental note to discuss my lack of sadness with Baba Valia, my grandma, when I got home. I was worried that maybe in my preschool upbringing, I had missed out on something else besides reading.

School got out early that day. On the tram ride home, I noted the ever-growing number of Soviet red flags going up around town. Black ribbons were attached to their tips. When I got off the tram and walked to my apartment, I saw that Pravdist also had a flag installed on its corner—it was blowing in the wind, a black ribbon skimming over its redness. For a moment I felt that the black ribbons might eventually make me sad.

I ran around the corner of my apartment building, a five-story structure lovingly known to its inhabitants as "the Sleeping Skyscraper" because of the multitude of its entrances and the sheer mass of brick that sprawled over the entire block. The Sleeping Skyscraper was built using a *khrushchevka* plan, named for Nikita Khrushchev, who had visited the northern port of Arkhangelsk in 1962 and decried the dismal living conditions in the wooden communal apartments. Studios and one-bedroom apartments in the Sleeping Skyscraper had indoor plumbing and running water. By 1982, our 474-square-foot, one-bedroom apartment housed my mom, Baba Valia, my younger brother and sister, myself, and our dog, a white Bolognese named Jacques.

I opened the heavy door of our entrance, ran up the first flight of stairs, and stopped at the row of blue mailboxes. I stuck my pinkie into the tiny round slot of mailbox #10 to check for mail. There was none. "Baba Valia must have picked it up already," I thought as I hopped up the concrete stairs to the third floor.

I rang the doorbell, and Baba Valia opened the door. The white fluff ball that was Jacques flew out from under her feet and jumped up and down until I petted him.

Baba Valia had moved to the Sleeping Skyscraper right after my parents' divorce in December 1980. With her arrival came hot lunches that filled the house with tummy-warming aromas, folded laundry, shoes neatly lined up in the hallway, and fairy tales at night—for me and my brother and sister. The taut grey curls of Baba Valia's perm bounced energetically as she quickly moved around our small apartment, always fetching something for one of us.

"Did you see all the black ribbons?" I asked.

"Yes, they always do that when the leader dies," Baba Valia said matter-of-factly, as if she knew that we all eventually become privy to the sacred ritual of a leader's death.

In the kitchen I dug in my schoolbag and pulled out my textbook to show Baba Valia my crooked black ribbon over Brezhnev's portrait.

"I messed up the ribbon," I said. "But you know what? Katia Kozlova cried when the teacher asked her to read about Leonid Il'ich Brezhnev today. But I didn't. I just couldn't, and I felt bad. Why didn't I?"

I searched for a hint of a reprimand in her deep grey eyes. But there was none.

"Well, I guess you had nothing to cry about," Baba Valia said thoughtfully. Even back then, when the contours of the reality that was my life were only coming into view, I sensed a certain aloofness in Baba Valia's attitude toward the government. It was as if she understood that things she couldn't do anything about, she had to let alone.

She reflected seriously on only one topic: the war. In the summer of 1942, when German planes bombed Arkhangelsk, Baba Valia was twenty-three. She spent the white summer nights dragging heavy buckets of sand up to the town's roofs and tossed the sand to snuff out the glistening lights of the incendiary bombs that Nazi Germans dropped on the city by the thousands. The wooden walkways of Arkhangelsk were swallowed by a rushing river of fire. Bread was rationed in tiny squares; that was why she still gathered all the breadcrumbs on the kitchen table by gently licking her finger and then picking them off the vinyl tablecloth. Peck, peck, peck her fingers would go as sweet bread disappeared on her tongue.

"So, who will be our leader now?" I asked.

"I don't know," she said, "but they will publish it in the newspaper soon."

A large portrait of Brezhnev covered a quarter of the front page of the next morning's paper. My mom scanned the front page. "Well, people are saying that Andropov might be the next in line. His name is listed first on the funeral organizing committee."

It was raining that day, and even when it stopped the next day, I stayed home—worried that it might be wrong to play outside. On the morning of November 13, the papers published the picture of the new leader. He had white hair, big glasses, and only one star on his black coat. The large letters under his picture read, "Yuri Vladimirovich Andropov."

I decided that I needed to remember the name of this new leader. I was not sure whether this was to cover for my lack of sadness about the passing of the previous one or just a conscious step to take my education into my own hands. The memorizing proved easy: "Yuri" was the name of the first Soviet cosmonaut, Gagarin; "Vladimirovich" was a patronymic derivative of Lenin's first name, Vladimir; and "Andropov" was only one letter different from the last name of my great-aunt, Antropov. And just in case, I had three more days to practice before school started.

Leonid Il'ich Brezhnev was buried two days later, on November 15, 1982, near the Kremlin wall, in a lavish state funeral. His many awards, fastened to crimson silk pillows, were carried by high military officers who marched with his coffin to his burial site in Red Square. Many world leaders sent their representatives or attended the funeral personally. For five minutes all the factories and offices in the Soviet Union stopped to mourn his passing. I stood next to the couch in our living room, still not sad but now more aware that we were supposed to behave in a certain way on such occasions.

2

WHO WANTS WAR?

APRIL 1983, ARKHANGELSK, USSR

It was the beginning of spring, a welcome season for a seven-year-old growing up in the Russian North. As I walked home from the tram stop, the tiny bits of ice still crunched under my rubber boots, and I was a little disappointed that not all the black puddles splashed back as I jumped on them. Yet the icicles on the Pravdist bookstore were getting shorter, and the trill they made as they dripped from the shop's awnings clearly sang of spring. The more experienced adults complained about all the grime the spring thaw brought up, but to me the tiny streams of melting snow stubbornly carving their paths through the spring slush signaled that soon it would be time to wear knee-highs to school and that summer was just around the corner.

One such a spring afternoon, as I was hanging up my coat in our apartment's narrow entryway, I noticed that Baba Valia seemed giddier than usual. She hurried into the kitchen and stood there wiping her hands on her apron, impatient for me to join her. She picked up a newspaper and shook it as if beckoning me to see for myself.

"There is an American girl who wrote a letter to the general secretary asking if the Soviets were going to start a nuclear war!" she said. "Can you imagine that?" Baba Valia was shocked and excited at the same time.

"What a strange question," I thought to myself. Why would we want to start a war? "I thought Americans were the ones who wanted to start a war, not us," I said.

"I know! What a question! Do they not know what the last war cost us?" Baba Valia asked, not really expecting me to answer.

"And so this girl wrote a letter to our General Secretary Andropov to ask him that?" I sat down at the kitchen table.

"Yes!"

"And?"

"Well, he wrote back to her, and they published the answer in today's paper. He told her that the Soviet people didn't want a war."

The general secretary wrote back to a girl? My interest was piqued. How was that possible? Was she just an ordinary girl? What was her name?

"Samantha Smith, it says here. And you know what he told her?" Baba Valia was on a roll. "'Come see for yourself,' he told her. He invited her to come to Camp Artek and meet our kids."

"Artek?!" I looked up at Baba Valia as she placed a bowl of hot soup in front of me.

Camp Artek was the most famous Soviet summer camp, a place every Soviet child dreamed of visiting. A child today might feel this way about Disney World or Universal Studios. But unlike the above locations, which require purchase of a ticket, a trip to Artek had to be earned. It was usually granted for great achievement in sports, school, or community and was the most coveted award a Soviet child could receive. Located in the Soviet resort area of Crimea, Artek was surrounded by tall mountains and sprawling cedar forests—where every dream of a perfect summer could come true: splashing in the salty Black Sea, looking for crabs along its rocky shores, hiking in the mountains, learning camp songs that only Artek campers knew, and maybe even catching a glimpse of some actors who, we heard, sometimes visited the camp. But most of all, we were curious about the international sessions in which campers could meet kids from other countries. None of us had ever met a foreigner before. We pondered how we could learn words in other languages and how we might teach them Russian.

Of course, I also knew how hard it was to get into Camp Artek. Rumors abounded about the highly competitive nature of the selection process. Some said you needed straight A's, but I knew many students with those grades who had never been there. Others said that on top of straight A's, you needed to be very involved in your school and community, to recycle newspapers, donate scrap metal, or do something else "for the benefit of the Motherland." No one would specify what that could be.

I worked hard in school, but my first-grade class was also a "sports class": half the students (myself included) were aspiring figure skaters; the other half were gymnasts—part of the government-sponsored athletic program. We were very busy first-graders. I had brought only one stack of newspapers for the recycled paper drive and no scrap metal at all.

In the early mornings I took a tram to the ice rink, where I met my classmates for a 7:00 a.m. practice, and then took another tram to school. There we navigated the still-dark school hallways to our classroom, where Nina Mikhailovna awaited us for "period zero," a special session that started before the other students got to school to allow us to finish earlier than the rest of our schoolmates. Several days a week I stayed for an afterschool program where I had lunch and did all my homework; then I followed my classmates and an afterschool teacher back to the ice rink for an evening training session at 5:00 p.m. Sometimes my mom picked me up at 7:00 p.m. for a bus ride back home; other times I went home on my own. Some days I was so tired, I fell asleep on the bus on my way home. Once I woke up at the final bus stop—in the unfamiliar part of town.

"Just stay on the bus. It goes in circles," advised an old lady in the seat nearby. "You will get to your stop eventually." I didn't let my eyes off the road until I saw that familiar bus stop on Suvorov Street.

Despite all the training sessions, I knew I was a long way from making any sizeable contribution to the world of sports—and hence the Motherland. My first school quarter I had five A's and four B's; the next quarter, four A's and five B's. There was no way I could go to Artek with grades like these. And yet this American girl had written to the general secretary asking such a strange question, and she got a response and an invitation to Artek?

"It's not fair," I told Baba Valia. "I'd need to get straight A's and collect a ton of scrap metal before they would even put my name on a list of kids to be considered for Artek. And even then I probably wouldn't be able to go, because we don't have, what do you and Mom call those—*connections*." I had picked up on the importance of connections very early in my life. My mom and Baba Valia said connections explained the reasons why some people had things we didn't, so I often wondered how one could get those connections.

"Hmm." Baba Valia was pondering my response.

"And imagine what would happen if I wrote a letter like that," I continued. "Mom would be called to the principal's office! And he would tell her what a bad daughter you two raised to ask such a question of the general secretary. You surely won't be packing me for Artek!"

"Well, she is an *American* girl!" Baba Valia said, as if implying that this might have qualified as a connection. "The paper says that she imagined Russians to be aliens from another planet! Don't you think she needs to see that we are not?"

"I suppose so," I thought. "But does this American girl have to go to Artek to see that we are not aliens?"

"American" in those days meant only one thing: enemy. Hence the two words "American girl" didn't quite fit together. A girl couldn't be an enemy in the same sense that the Nazi Germans were during the Great Patriotic War (as World War II was known in the Soviet Union), bombing our towns and killing our people. Nazis were the only other example I could think of when I heard the word "enemy." And if the girl was an enemy, however that was possible, why did the general secretary invite her to Artek? It didn't make any sense.

Making the whole situation even worse was that I, too, would soon be going to a summer camp. My mom, like many parents from the northern Soviet cities, cherished an opportunity to send her child down south for the summer "to swim in the sea and to soak up the sun for the long winter ahead." Forty-five days was a typical length of stay. The summer camps in my day were referred to as pioneer camps, so named after the Pioneer Organization, started after the 1917 revolution to replace the popular Boy and Girl Scout clubs. While excited by the prospect of a trip to the sea, I knew that the camp I'd be going to, called Gaidarovets, would be nothing like Artek.

Gaidarovets meant a follower of Gaidar, the famous Soviet children's book author Arkady Gaidar. One of his short stories, "Conscience," was a favorite of Nina Mikhailovna's. It was about her namesake, a girl named Nina, who skipped school one day because she hadn't done her homework. To avoid being discovered, Nina went to the woods, where she hid her books and lunch and chased a butterfly. When she stumbled on a little kid who was afraid of a big dog wandering in the woods, she felt sorry for him and walked him home. When Nina finally got back to her books, she saw that the big dog had eaten her lunch. She sat down and cried—not because she had lost her lunch but because she felt guilty about skipping school.

"You must always listen to the voice of your conscience," Nina Mikhailovna admonished us. I never skipped school, and I disliked the lessons Nina Mikhailovna seemed to find in every short story. They made me feel guilty even though I'd done nothing wrong.

There would be a sea near Gaidarovets, I was told, but none of the other things I imagined Artek would have. And there would be no kids from other countries that I was curious about. Come July, my mother would make a list of my clothes on a piece of notebook paper, which she would then glue to the inside of my hard-shell suitcase. To ensure that what little clothing I had would return home safely, my mother would type "Lena Pravilova" over and over again on a long piece of cotton cloth on a typewriter during her lunch break at the local engineering firm. Baba Valia then would cut the cloth into tiny nametags and sew them on my dresses, shirts, skirts, and underwear and even inside my socks.

It seemed unfair that an American girl was invited to Artek because she wrote a letter asking a question that made so little sense and I would have to go to a camp named Gaidarovets.

How could anyone think we wanted to start a war? Baba Valia always wiped away tears when they showed war movies on TV. The Soviet war movies were so sad that Baba Valia wouldn't let me watch some of them. When the TV broadcast the May 9 Victory concerts, she'd turn up the volume. Usually gentle and comforting, she sat frozen and unapproachable as the singer's voice thundered,

Arise, the vast country,
Rise up for the mortal fight
With German horde uncounted,
With forces of the night.

"Oh, how I remember our boys marching away," she would sigh. I wanted to know whom she remembered, what flashed before her eyes, and why she looked like she was about to cry. But I was afraid to ask.

There was another song Baba Valia liked. The deep, sad voice of her favorite singer, Mark Bernes, asked and answered the question "The Russians, do they want war?"

Ask the silence that hovers
over our plowed fields and plains,
ask birches, ask poplars.
Just ask the soldiers
who lie beneath the birches!
The sons will answer for their fathers:
whether the Russians really want war.

"Hasn't this girl heard the song?" I wondered, completely unaware of the distance that separated us. I liked that song very much—both its melody and its lyrics. "Russians don't want war," it said. That, of course, begged a question: Who does?

At school Nina Mikhailovna had the answer: "The Americans and their President Ronald Reagan want to start a nuclear war. Nuclear weapons are scarier than any other weapons in the world. All of us would be gone in an instant."

I searched for a picture of Ronald Reagan in the newspapers my family subscribed to, as I wanted to see the face of the crazy man who wanted to start another war. I found only caricatures of a tall man, wearing a top hat with stars and stripes on it; he had a witchlike nose and held a finger on a big button labeled "Nuclear Bomb." Smirking at me from the page, he seemed ready to press it at any moment.

3

"WHY DON'T *YOU*?"

APRIL 11, 1983, MANCHESTER, MAINE

The chilly morning of April 11, 1983, started like any other Monday in the Smith household on Worthing Road in Manchester, Maine. As usual, Jane was the first to get up and the first to head out the door. She knew that Arthur, who taught classes later that day, would make sure Samantha ate breakfast and caught the school bus on time. She kissed the two of them and then drove the six miles to her office at the Maine Department of Human Services in Augusta. On her way in, she grabbed a coffee and an English muffin at the snack bar—to eat at her desk. Later that morning, she had a three-hour drive to Machias for a meeting. As a residential services contract manager, she was used to long drives. That day, she took "the airline"—a rural road cutting across Maine west to east—to avoid the coastal traffic, ate lunch in her car, attended the meeting, and then set out for home. It was almost 8:00 p.m. when she drove into their garage. She was exhausted and starving.

Yet, when she saw Arthur waiting for her in the garage, looking very excited, she suspected that she had missed something big.

"Do you remember that letter Sam wrote to the Kremlin?"

"Hmm . . . yes."

"The Soviets published it in *Pravda*, and Channel 8 is coming to interview Sam in a few minutes!"

"What???!!"

Jane remembered a weekend morning a few months earlier, when Sam came into the living room with that big question: "Mom, are we going to have a war?" Jane had let her watch a science show about nuclear war on public television the night before. The narrator told of the radioactive fallout that would poison the atmosphere and the terrible fate that awaited those who survived such a cataclysm. Jane briefly considered turning it off, but Sam was curious, and so she let her finish. The images must have crept into Sam's dreams that night, and the next morning she couldn't quite shake them off.

Jane picked up the *Time* magazine from the coffee table. Its cover pictured the new Soviet leader, Yuri Andropov. She had read the magazine the day before and now tried to explain the complexities of Soviet-American relations to her ten-year-old daughter. The November 22, 1982, issue, titled "After Brezhnev: Andropov Takes Command," detailed the elaborate funeral preparations for the previous Soviet leader, Leonid Brezhnev. One article pondered what course Andropov, "a witty conversationalist, a bibliophile, a connoisseur of modern art . . . [and] the former boss of the world's most powerful and possibly most feared police organization," would choose for his country. It talked about the nuclear stockpiles that both sides had: "The U.S.S.R. and the U.S. now possess approximately the same number of ballistic missile warheads—more than 7,000. These warheads are the fastest, most accurate and destructive long-range weapons in the two sides' arsenals of last resort. In Soviet eyes, they symbolize the U.S.S.R.'s attainment of equality with the U.S. as a superpower."

"This is the new Soviet leader." Jane pointed at the picture on the cover. "I sure hope he might be the one to figure out how our two countries could get along."

"Do the Soviets have a lot of nuclear bombs?" Sam asked.

"Yes," Jane replied.

"Do we have nuclear bombs?" Sam continued.

"Yes."

"So we are making the bombs to protect ourselves from the Soviets and . . . they are making the bombs to protect themselves from us?" Sam asked.

"It sure seems like that," Jane answered.

"That's so dumb," Sam said. "Why would anyone want a nuclear war?" She furrowed her eyebrows and looked down as she often did when deep in thought, intently searching for an answer among her toes. Then her face lit up. "Why doesn't somebody just write to their leader and ask if he is going to have a war?"

Sam looked up at Jane. "Mom, can you just write to him and ask him?"

"Why don't *you* write to him?" Jane suggested.

Sam was not new to letter writing. When she was five and they lived in Amity, a tiny Maine town on the border with Canada, Arthur, then an English instructor at Ricker College, often brought little Sam along to his classes when they couldn't find a babysitter. Sam usually sat at the back of the classroom and worked on her coloring book. For one of his assignments, Arthur had his students write a letter to someone important. They were to explain a thought, right a wrong, get money back, or convince someone of something—the object could be persuasion or to just to express one's feelings. He believed that letter writing was a useful life skill.

Sam was clearly paying attention. When the summer of 1977 heralded Queen Elizabeth II's silver jubilee, Canada's CBC (one of three television channels the Smiths got in Amity) broadcast the lavish celebrations in London and the queen's tour of the Commonwealth. Canada was the last stop of the royal tour, and Prince Charles joined the queen and Prince Philip in greeting the crowds. Sam was glued to the TV, awestruck by the pageantry. Then, out of the blue, she said she wanted to write to the queen to tell her that she had seen her on TV and liked her very much. And she did just that. Arthur helped her address the envelope:

Queen Elizabeth II
Buckingham Palace
London, England

Weeks later, a thank-you note from the queen's lady-in-waiting arrived addressed to Miss Samantha Smith. Sam was elated. Arthur was proud.

Dear Mr. Andropov,

My name is Samantha Smith.
I am 10 years old.
Congragulations on your new job.
I have been worrying about Russia
and The United States getting into a
Nuculear war. Are you going to vote to have
a war or not? If you aren't please tell
me how you are going to help to not
have a war. This question you do
not have to answer but I would like
it if you would. Why do you want to
conquer the world or at least our
country? God made the world for us
to share and take care of. Not to fight
over or have one group of people own
it all. Please lets do what he wanted
and have every body be happy too.

Samantha Smith
Manchester, Maine U.S.A.
Box 44
04351

P.S. Please write back.

Samantha's letter to Yuri Andropov. Federal Archive Agency. 2014. http://archives
.gov.ru/index.php?q=exhibitions/2014-andropov_press.shtml.

So when Jane suggested that Sam write a letter to the new Soviet leader Yuri Andropov, Sam already knew what to do. She went to her room and produced the following:

Dear Mr. Andropov,
My name is Samantha Smith.
I am 10 years old.
    Congragulations [sic] on your new job. I have been worrying about Russia and The United States getting into a Nuculear [sic] war. Are you going to vote to have a war or not? If you aren't please tell me how you are going to help to not have a war. This question you do not have to answer but I would like it if you would. Why do you want to conquer the world or at least our country? God made the world for us to share and take care of. Not to fight over or have one group of people own it all. Please let's do what he wanted and have every body [sic] be happy too.
Samantha Smith
Manchester, Maine U.S.A.
Box 44
04351
P.S. Please write back.

Jane helped her address the letter:

Mr. Yuri Andropov
The Kremlin
Moscow
USSR

Arthur took Sam to the post office to mail the letter. She was very surprised that the stamp for a letter going to the Soviet Union cost forty cents instead of the usual twenty cents. Weeks went by with no reply, and soon they forgot about this exercise in civic participation—that is, until the phone rang at Manchester Elementary on Monday morning, April 11, with a United Press International reporter asking for Samantha Smith.

"Mrs. Peabody appeared in the doorway and asked me to follow her to the office," Sam recounted that morning's events. "There must be some mistake, I said. And she asked, 'Well, did you write a letter or something to Yuri Andropov? There is a reporter on the phone for you.' She practically dragged me into her office and then she just handed me the phone."

"What did the reporter say?" Jane asked Sam.

"She asked if I wrote the letter to the Kremlin and told me that the Soviets had printed it in *Pravda*. She wanted to know why I wrote the letter. I said I was worried about the nuclear war between the US and the Soviet Union. She asked me if I've heard back from Andropov. I haven't, I said. And then I asked if she knew whether he planned to write back. She didn't know."

The *Kennebec Journal* had already been to the house to interview Sam, Arthur said. They had even taken a picture of Sam for the paper.

"My goodness, I sure missed a lot! When did you say the TV crew was coming?" Jane asked, figuring that she'd need to straighten up and maybe grab a bite.

Thirty minutes later, a WMTW Channel 8 TV crew pulled up to their house.

4

"MY AGE HAS NOTHING TO DO WITH IT"

APRIL 1983, MANCHESTER, MAINE

The next morning's issue of the *Kennebec Journal* announced America's youngest diplomat. The picture showed Sam grinning and posing next to Arthur's typewriter. At around 6:00 p.m., they went next door, to the Dunns' house, to watch the Channel 8 broadcast of Sam's interview in color. When Sam appeared on TV, answering questions about her letter to the Kremlin, Jane was taken aback by how well she handled herself. It seemed that just last week Sam had been giggling so hard with her friend Susan Brann that Jane wondered whether her daughter could even speak in complete sentences. Now the ten-year-old seemed so poised and articulate. Jane felt tears well up in her eyes.

She looked at Sam, who also seemed to be wiping away tears.

"What are you crying about, silly? You did a great job!" she said.

A few days later, Arthur managed to locate a copy of *Pravda* and asked his Russian-speaking colleagues at the University of Maine to translate it. Samantha's letter was reproduced in an April 11, 1983, *Pravda* feature titled "Concern, Hopes, Wishes: Letters to Y. V. Andropov from across the Ocean." A large spread on page four praised Andropov's peace initiative and quoted letters the Soviet leader had received from the West. The article seemingly alluded to an earlier controversial *Pravda* piece published on February 22 that also quoted letters from the West praising Andropov's stance on peace. That issue provided no photographs, and the *New York Times* accused *Pravda* of manufacturing the names. In this issue, *Pravda* included a photograph showing about a dozen letters spread out on a table. Sam's letter, most of her elementary school scrawl easily readable, took up about a quarter of the shot.

Thirty-one years later, in 2014, it took me much longer to locate that copy of *Pravda*, and then, almost simultaneously, I received two copies—one from the Maine State Museum and one from a faithful website follower in Russia who had managed to get a copy from her local library. *Pravda*, translated as "truth," was the official newspaper of the Communist Party of the Soviet Union. Along with its counterpart, *Izvestia* (meaning "news"), the official organ of the Soviet government, it was entrusted with hammering out government propaganda on a daily basis. A saying that originated among the Soviets themselves was frequently thrown around by foreigners with respect to the two Soviet papers: "In the *Truth*, there is no news, and in the *News*, there is no truth." Despite the papers' high circulation rates, their intended audiences didn't have much confidence in them.

Samantha wasn't the only person to write to Yuri Andropov that year. "A multitude of new letters from US citizens, addressed to the Soviet leader, still continue to arrive," *Pravda* claimed. *Pravda* quoted some of the correspondents. Walter Kaiser, a veteran with the American Legion Paradise Post 79 in New Port Richey, Florida, was impressed by Andropov's unprecedented and much-publicized Q&A sessions with the American journalist Joseph Kingsbury-Smith. Other authors, *Pravda* editors claimed, were "reasonable for the most part" but nonetheless seemed to make some ridiculous claims. Citing a line from Sam's letter—"Why do you want to conquer the whole world or at least our country?"—*Pravda* smirked, "We think we can pardon Samantha for her misconceptions because the girl is only 10 years old."

Soon the news of Sam's letter appearing in *Pravda* was in newspapers across the United States. Relatives and friends in Virginia and Florida collected the clippings and mailed them to Maine. Arthur pinned them on the wall in his office. Sam was excited but also curious as to why

Andropov had not responded. This particularly bothered her after she learned that the *Pravda* editors had seemed to make fun of her age. Both Jane and Arthur tried to explain that governments did such things with an ulterior motive, that the Soviets might be using her letter and that of others as propaganda to promote their purportedly peace-loving attitudes.

"Every side would like to believe they are peace-loving," proposed Arthur.

But Jane and Arthur both also thought that getting to the bottom of things might be a great educational experience for Sam. When it came to getting answers to big questions, this seemed a good opportunity. So, being supportive, Arthur suggested Sam write to the Soviet ambassador to the United States, Anatoly Dobrynin. He found the address of the Soviet embassy, and Sam sat down to write another letter, this time typing it on her father's typewriter.

April 13, 1983
P.O. Box 44
Manchester, ME
04351
Dear Mr. Ambassador,

Afew [sic] months ago I wrote to Mr. Yuri Andropov, and asked him some polite questions. He has not responded. But your Russian newspaper (Pravda) did show some parts of my letter.

They said I was forgiven for asking that question just because Iam [sic] only ten years old. Ithink [sic] that my questions were good questions to ask and my age has nothing to do with it. I am disappointed that he has not written back to me.

Could you tell me please if the Russian children think like I do?

If there is no war I hope I can visit Russia someday.

Thankyou [sic] very much. Please write back.

Sincerly [sic],

Samantha R. Smith

A week later, the phone rang at their house in Manchester. Sam picked it up. A heavily accented voice inquired whether he had reached the Smith residence. At first she thought it was one of her dad's friends playing a joke on her, now that everyone knew she had written to the Soviet Union.

"I am calling to inform you that the letter from the general secretary of the Central Committee of the Communist Party, Yuri Andropov, is on its way," the man said. He then dictated several phone numbers, which Sam wrote down—just in case. He asked her to notify the embassy when the letter arrived so that the Soviets could release the information to the news networks. When Arthur got home, he called the FBI office in Augusta to check the numbers and received confirmation that they indeed were for the Soviet embassy in Washington, DC.

On the morning of April 25, 1983, two weeks after Sam's letter first appeared in *Pravda*, the phone rang yet again. This time it was Alice, the postmaster, saying that a strange envelope addressed to Samantha Smith had just arrived.

Instead of taking the school bus that morning, Sam climbed into Arthur's red Toyota Celica to go to the post office. She wanted to get a glimpse of the letter before heading off to school.

The letter from Andropov, dated April 19, 1983, was typed on cream-colored paper and signed in blue ink. It was accompanied by an English translation. Sam had only a few minutes to read it on the way to school, but she did notice Andropov's invitation to visit the Soviet Union.

"Can we go?" she asked.

"We'll see," was Arthur's reply—the reply he usually gave before he said yes.

He wouldn't let her take the letter to school, fearing she'd lose it. When he got home, Arthur called the Soviet embassy to notify them of the letter's arrival. The Soviets then released the news to the media.

By the time Jane got home from work that evening, she could barely recognize their house. There were reporters all over their front lawn and inside their home as well. They wanted pictures of the whole family on the front porch stairs and one of Sam holding Andropov's letter at the kitchen table. When someone suggested Samantha read Andropov's letter at her father's desk, she obliged, her finger following the words as she read.

Dear Samantha,

I received your letter, which is like many others that have reached me recently from your country and from other countries around the world.

It seems to me—I can tell by your letter—that you are a courageous and honest girl, resembling Becky, the friend of Tom Sawyer in the famous book of your compatriot Mark Twain. This book is well known and loved in our country by all boys and girls.

You write that you are anxious about whether there will be a nuclear war between our two countries. And you ask are we doing anything so that war will not break out.

Your question is the most important of those that every thinking man can pose. I will reply to you seriously and honestly.

Yes, Samantha, we in the Soviet Union are trying to do everything so that there will not be war between our countries, so that in general there will not be war on earth. This is what every Soviet man wants. This is what the great founder of our state, Vladimir Lenin, taught us.

Soviet people well know what a terrible thing war is. Forty-two years ago, Nazi Germany, which strived for supremacy over the whole world, attacked our country, burned and destroyed many thousands of our towns and villages, killed millions of Soviet men, women and children.

In that war, which ended with our victory, we were in alliance with the United States: together we fought for the liberation of many people from the Nazi invaders. I hope that you know about this from your history lessons in school. And today we want very much to live in peace, to trade and cooperate with all our neighbors on this earth— with those far away and those nearby. And certainly, with such a great country as the United States of America.

In America and in our country, there are nuclear weapons—terrible weapons that can kill millions of people in an instant. But we do not want them ever to be used. That's precisely why the Soviet Union solemnly declared throughout the entire world that never—never—will it use nuclear weapons first against any country. In general we propose to discontinue further production of them and to proceed to the abolition of all the stockpiles on earth.

It seems to me that this is a sufficient answer to your second question: "Why do you want to wage war against the whole world or at least the United States?" We want nothing of the kind. No one in our country—neither workers, peasants, writers nor doctors, neither grown-ups nor children, nor members of the government—want either a big or "little" war.

We want peace—there is something that we are occupied with: growing wheat, building and inventing, writing books and flying into space. We want peace for ourselves and for all peoples of the planet. For our children and for you, Samantha.

I invite you, if your parents will let you, to come to our country, the best time being this summer. You will find out about our country, meet with your contemporaries, visit an international children's camp—"Artek"—on the sea. And see for yourself: in the Soviet Union, everyone is for peace and friendship among peoples.

Thank you for your letter. I wish you all the best in your young life.

Y. Andropov

"What do you think about Andropov comparing you to Becky Thatcher, a famous heroine of Mark Twain's *Tom Sawyer?*" asked one of the reporters.

Jane and Arthur thought the comparison clever, although they wondered whether Andropov expected all Americans to have read Twain. Sam said she took it as a compliment and added, "When you think of Yuri Andropov, you really don't think about him having any humor."

Then the reporters turned to Jane and Arthur. "What did you think of your daughter's correspondence?"

Arthur shook his head. "This is just entirely unbelievable. Nations do things for political reasons. Andropov obviously didn't write to her simply because he's one of her fans." Although skeptical about the Soviet leader's true intentions, Jane and Arthur thought that the message sounded genuine.

That same evening, a chartered plane was arranged to fly Jane and Sam to New York City. Sam had invitations to appear on *The Today Show* and the *CBS Morning News* the next morning.

5

LIVE ON NATIONAL TV

APRIL 1983, NEW YORK CITY, NEW YORK

Before they could leave for the airport, the phone rang again. ABC's *Nightline* lead booking producer, Tara Sonenshine, was on the line. *Nightline*, a thirty-minute late-night show well known for its cutting-edge mix of investigative journalism and interviews, wanted Sam to appear on the program that very night. She would be one of its youngest guests.

Jane didn't know what to say.

"Samantha would love to do it, but she is going to appear on *The Today Show* tomorrow morning."

"Where are you staying?" Sonenshine persisted. NBC had booked them a room at the Mayflower Hotel in Manhattan, Jane replied.

"I'll be there to meet you," Sonenshine said.

When Jane and Sam arrived at their hotel at 10:30 p.m., Sonenshine, a one-woman welcoming crew, was waiting for them in the lobby. Young and lively, she talked of the *Nightline* opportunity. There would be a different audience from the one watching *The Today Show* in the morning. They would also have pizza and ice cream in the green room. Jane looked over at Sam and noticed that the last detail seemed to have sealed the deal—Sam was really excited despite the late hour. Not having too much time to ponder the proposition, they hopped into the studio limousine.

It was past 11:00 p.m. when they pulled up to the ABC News building, and Sam was immediately whisked away to a studio with only minutes before going on air. The show's host, Ted Koppel, would be interviewing her remotely from the *Nightline* studio in Washington, DC. Jane was directed to another room in the building where she could watch Sam on a monitor. The ABC studios seemed very confusing to her—everyone was in different rooms, connected through monitors and wires.

But the hour was late, and she didn't consider it for long. This was Sam's first time on national TV, and it was going to be live. Jane was nervous.

Yet, as she watched the monitor, she could see that Sam wasn't the least bit concerned. And Jane knew it wasn't just the promise of pizza and ice cream that had worked their magic. Since the day Sam's letter appeared in *Pravda*, both she and Arthur had been impressed with Sam's easygoing attitude about the media attention.

"When she got off the school bus," Arthur told Jane earlier in the day, "the reporters started shouting out questions: 'Why did you write to Mr. Andropov? Did you expect Mr. Andropov to answer your letter? Will you go to the USSR? What do you think of all this?' She seemed completely unfazed—she paused, looked around, answered a couple of questions, and kept walking towards the house as if this was something she did every day."

Sam had always been an easygoing kid. Even as a baby, when she crawled or walked into their room early in the morning, she always had a big smile on her face, as if to say, "Gosh, I'm *so* happy to see you." But she was also shy; just a few months earlier, she had been too timid to audition for a part in the school play, and she avoided chatting with Jane's friends when they were visiting. So as Jane watched the blue *Nightline* logo rise across the screen and the show's host Ted Koppel introduce Sam, she held her breath.

"And, finally, tonight the story of Samantha Smith, a ten-year-old girl from Manchester, Maine. Earlier this year, Samantha wrote a letter to Soviet leader Yuri Andropov. She congratulated him on becoming a head of the Soviet Communist Party and asked him some questions about Soviet attitude towards the United States."

Jane watched Sam's grinning face appear on the large newsroom monitor behind Koppel. She wiggled in her chair and looked around the peculiar set awaiting the first question.

"Samantha, you've got quite a pen pal there! What did he write to you?" Koppel asked.

"Well, he said, that I resembled Becky Thatcher in ... the [book] *Tom Sawyer*," Sam replied, her voice going hoarse from all the talking that day.

Koppel asked whether she sent him a picture.

"No, I didn't. He said I was courageous."

"Well, that you were. But let's begin at the beginning. What did you write to him, and what did he write back?" asked Koppel.

"Well, I asked him, why do you want to conquer the world? And he wrote back to me and said that he wanted nothing of the kind and gave me a little history lesson on the last war they had. And he said that he didn't want to have a war or anything like that again."

Koppel wanted to know more.

"Well, I asked him who would start the war first," she said.

"Not him, I'll bet," Koppel said.

"Yeah. He said that if we were going to have a war, they would never be the first ones to start it."

"Well, now that you've gone through this experience, and I must say it's one of the more effective exercises in diplomacy that we've seen in this country in quite a while—now that you've completed it, what do you conclude from all of this?" Koppel asked.

"Well, I just hope we can have peace, and I hope it'll do some good."

6

JANIE

Some might say that Jane had always had an independent streak—not what one expected of a minister's daughter. But then her father wasn't your run-of-the-mill minister. "If there are people who would rather read a book than go out, he wasn't that type of man," Jane's younger brother Hank would say of their father years later.

The years of the Great Depression had toughened Donald Goshorn, and he admired resourcefulness and perseverance in others. In 1929, when the Wall Street crisis forced many college students to leave school in search of work, Donald didn't abandon his education. It would take another eight years, three different schools, several jobs in between, and a move to Dallas, Texas, to live with his aunt and uncle while he earned a degree in psychology from Southern Methodist University. He then entered the Union Presbyterian Seminary in Richmond, Virginia.

In Richmond, Donald met his future wife, Jane Larus Reed, a graduate of the King Smith private school in Washington, DC. The youngest of seven siblings in the well-known Reed family of Richmond, petite Jane hardly noticed the Depression. Yet tragedy didn't pass the family by. On April 10, 1935, Jane's seventeenth birthday, her mother passed away, leaving her to take care of the house and her ailing father. Donald and Jane got married in November 1941, and soon the young Reverend and Mrs. Goshorn started pastoring four small churches in western Virginia. During World War II, Donald served in the US Navy as a chaplain.

Donald and Jane's first child, Jane—or Janie, as she would soon become known to avoid confusing her with her mother and a cousin, also named Jane—was born in 1944. Janie's younger brother, named after his father but known in the family as Hank, arrived in 1948.

Reverend Goshorn, an avid sportsman, horseman, acrobat, and swimmer, was determined to share his love of the outdoors with his daughter. In the summers, when they visited relatives on Mattaponi River in eastern Virginia, Janie could be seen in tall rubber boots sloshing knee-deep in water alongside her father as the two climbed inside a little row-boat to go fly-fishing for the day.

On her seventh birthday, Janie received a BB gun as a gift from her dad and immediately wanted to know how it worked. After checking to see that the barrel was empty, her dad put his hand over the muzzle and then pulled the trigger two times, explaining how the air felt on his hand when he fired a shot. Her dad had told her to never point a gun at a person, so she was confused.

"What do you mean?" Janie asked.

"Do you want to try?" he asked.

She wasn't so sure at first but then nodded. He let her put her little hand over the muzzle and pulled the trigger again. Startled, Janie pulled her hand back, ran to the couch, and buried her head in the pillows, crying.

"It didn't hurt that much, did it?" her father asked.

When Janie finally opened her hand, she revealed a pool of blood in her palm. A BB, stuck during the two firings, had finally come free. Brother Hank was swiftly taken to the neighbor, and Janie was rushed to the doctor, who removed the BB and sewed up the hand. The real test, of course, came the next Sunday at church when Reverend and Mrs. Goshorn had to explain the thick bandage on Janie's hand. Yet the incident didn't deter her, and soon she became a great marksperson.

At Camp Lachlan, where Janie spent her summers, she took horse-riding lessons. One summer, on a family visit to Richmond, she was anxious to share what she'd learned with her older cousin Edie. The two girls climbed on the horses and took off. Things were going quite well until the two of them hopped over a small, downed tree in their path, and the stirrup came disconnected from Janie's saddle, causing her to fall. As horse people were taught to do, Janie "got right back on the horse." And she was fine, except for a cut on her head, which bled and required three stitches. Janie continued to practice and over time became a better rider, in the ring and on the fox hunt course, eventually bringing home a few ribbons and trophies. As a teen, she returned to Camp Lachlan as a rifle and riding instructor.

The family moved seven times during Janie's childhood, but both she and her brother took the moves in stride—Hank, happy to start up at a new location with a clean slate; Janie, always up for a challenge. In 1960, when she was in tenth grade, the family moved to pastor a new church in Cheriton, Virginia. The Holmes Presbyterian Church had been looking for a pastor willing to remain in the area for a few years. Since the Eastern Shore proved a dull setting for recent seminary graduates, the church had to search for a new pastor at regular intervals. When a church member noticed a boat tied to the top of Reverend Goshorn's car, she concluded, "This one is going to stay." And she was right.

In September 1962, Janie started at Hollins College in Roanoke, Virginia, an all-girls school. She did look at other schools—but not too seriously. Several cousins went to Hollins and told her about Tinker Day, which sold her on the school. On a random morning in autumn, the college president would ring the campus and chapel bells, stand on the steps of the main building, and declare all classes cancelled. Then students and faculty would climb the nearby Tinker Mountain for a picnic and festivities.

Janie, who now went by Jane, quickly settled into her studies as an art major at Hollins, where she met her lifelong friends Amanda Chase, Diana Cunningham, and Kay Kendall. The all-girls school was small, and the belief that "women can do anything" agreed with Jane very much.

In the spring of her sophomore year in 1964, Jane persuaded her parents to let her join some classmates and a philosophy professor, Allie Frazier, on a trip to Europe. She had not signed up for Hollins Abroad, a program that offered a whole semester of study abroad, and now really wanted to go in the summer. The tour was a whirlwind—twelve European cities in two weeks. It included, at the request of one of her more outgoing classmates, a stop in the Soviet Union.

Years later, she remembered best from that trip their arrival in Warsaw, Poland. It coincided with that of the boisterous Soviet premier

Nikita Khrushchev, who was in town for the twentieth anniversary of the People's Polish Republic. On hearing that the Soviet leader was giving a speech at the large city square, the girls followed their guide and chaperones through the city streets to catch a glimpse of the premier.

At the square, dense crowds stretched for blocks. Jane took a picture of a sign that declared, "Socialism will win all over the world." She continued snapping pictures as the sea of people kept pushing her and her friends toward the front of the crowd. Soldiers marched first in the parade. Planes flew in formations overhead, and trucks, tanks, and other military equipment drove past. Students marched carrying portraits of Karl Marx, Vladimir Lenin, and Khrushchev. A boy in the crowd offered help—he knew a place from which they could see Khrushchev, he said. Jane and her group pushed through the crowd, walked over benches, crossed the street, and went through the bushes, arriving at the tallest building in Warsaw. Now in the very front row, Jane had an almost unobstructed view of the tall platform where all the dignitaries gathered. She watched the Soviet premier as he waved at the parade of tanks and other military equipment going by. When he spoke, Jane didn't understand a word, but for a moment she was sure he was looking right at her.

Their next stop was Moscow, the capital of the Soviet Union. In the summer of 1964, Moscow looked grey and dreary, despite the glitter of the city's museums and the vastness of its monuments. The brief period known as the "Khrushchev Thaw" was drawing to a close. A decade earlier, Khrushchev had denounced Joseph Stalin's repressions and relaxed every sphere of Soviet life. The "thaw" also heralded a somewhat warmer atmosphere in US-Soviet relations, but they soon worsened again when the Soviets shot down an American U-2 reconnaissance plane in 1960. Khrushchev took personal offense at American unwillingness to admit that it was a spy plane, and this incident resulted in a huge blow to his trust in the West.

The girls were mostly confined to the posh Hotel Ukraina, likened to "a wedding cake" for its stacked tiers of floors. They saw only art museums, theaters, foreigners, waiters, and their dour tour guide. Jane loved the Moscow metro, noting its fast escalators, marble walls, chandeliers, statues, and mosaics throughout. They also traveled to Leningrad, where they visited the Hermitage Museum and Jane took copious notes for her art classes.

On their group's arrival in Helsinki the next day, she wrote in her journal, "Amazing feeling of relief to be FREE again."

In the fall of her senior year at Hollins, Jane got an unexpected call from Arthur Smith, an English teacher at nearby Radford College. He was inviting her on a date. He said he was friends with her cousin Bill Goshorn. Jane had heard about two teachers at Radford who had dated her classmates. She knew both were considered acceptable dates; yet one was in his forties, which in Jane's mind seemed way too old for her. Nevertheless, she accepted the date, hoping Arthur Smith was the younger one. Then she rushed to find a classmate to ask her whether she would meet the older or the younger.

Arthur Smith turned out to be the younger one, only four years older than she. On their first date, Jane was charmed by his intellect, good looks, and great sense of humor, especially his habit of saying something in jest while assuming a mock serious look and raising one eyebrow way up, signifying humor and eliciting laughter. Arthur was an academic who loved poetry and literature of all kinds; he played classical guitar but also loved race cars. It was a charmingly unusual combination.

Jane graduated from Hollins in June 1966 and moved to New York, where she spent a year working as a Pan Am stewardess, which then was a great opportunity to travel and see the world. Jane and Arthur were married in May 1967 at the Holmes Presbyterian Church in Cheriton, Virginia, with her father, Reverend Goshorn, officiating. In the fall of that year, they moved to Pittsburgh, Pennsylvania, where Arthur was accepted into graduate school at the University of Pittsburgh with a teaching fellowship in the English Department.

In the summer of 1971, they packed up once more. With their Irish wolfhound Gar and their cat Ford, they drove north on I-95 to Houlton, Maine, where Arthur was to start as an English instructor at Ricker College. They bought a house outside Houlton, with acres of fields for Gar to play in, and in late fall of 1971, they had some good news to report to their families: they were expecting their first child in June.

Samantha Reed Smith arrived at 1:45 p.m. on a windy Thursday, June 29, 1972, in Houlton. A few days later, Jane and Arthur drove their baby girl home to a small town named Amity, which means "friendship among peoples."

7

"ARE YOU TIRED OF ANSWERING ALL THESE QUESTIONS?"

APRIL 1983, LOS ANGELES, CALIFORNIA

Four days after Andropov's letter arrived, Jane and Sam were bound for California, where Sam was scheduled to appear on *The Tonight Show Starring Johnny Carson*. On the plane, Sam and her best friend, Lynn D'Avanzo, planned out their visit to Disneyland, which *The Tonight Show* had included on their itinerary. Sam wanted to share her adventure with her best friend. Jane remembered how happy she was when Sam met Lynn on her softball team when they moved away from Amity. The two became quick friends, much to Jane's delight.

Their move to Manchester was initially hard on Sam.

"No one likes me here!" Sam declared when she got home from her first day at Manchester Elementary. Worried, Jane scrambled to see what she could do to fix the situation. She signed Sam up for softball and gymnastics and then resurrected a Brownie troop at Manchester Elementary to help Sam get to know kids better outside school.

Lynn D'Avanzo was "a hoot, cute, tiny, and intense." A dynamo of a girl with a great sense of humor, Lynn, who was a pitcher on the team, would "sometimes try to play all over the field—as if the other players were too slow, and she had to do it all." "She was hilarious to watch, a one-girl action show," Jane would remember years later. Sam and Lynn loved to hike in the woods behind the Smiths' house, where they followed the creek in hopes of finding its end. They played dress-up, trying on Jane's college dresses and stuffing the bodices full of tissue paper to fill out their bosoms. They got their ears pierced on the same day.

On the evening of April 29, 1983, the guest list for *The Tonight Show Starring Johnny Carson* included Jennifer Beals of *Flashdance* fame and Samantha Smith of Manchester, Maine. Jane and Lynn sat on the couch in the green room watching Sam on the studio monitor. When Johnny Carson announced her name, Sam, dressed in a white polka-dotted turtleneck and Levi's, marched onto the stage. She shook Carson's hand and took her seat in the large, plush chair next to his desk. Her feet dangled, unable to reach the floor.

"Are you getting tired of answering all the questions that people like myself and people on the news shows are asking you?" he asked.

"Yes," Sam replied with a grin. The audience, along with the host, erupted in laughter.

"How did you get the idea to write the letter?" Carson asked.

"Well, nuclear war was on TV a lot lately, and it got so steady on TV that I got scared," Samantha answered.

"Did you ever expect in your wildest imagination that you would get a reply?" asked Carson.

"Yeah, hopefully just a small friendly letter back." Sam shrugged her shoulders.

"So he said he didn't want another war. Well, they suffered greatly in the Second World War," said Carson. "They didn't want another one. Did you feel better after you got this reply?" asked Carson.

"Yes, I really did," Sam replied.

"Did you believe him? Do you think he means what he says?"

"Yeah," she answered.

"I think the Soviet leaders have children and they have grandchildren, and I think when they come out and say that they don't want nuclear war, that is probably in their best interest too, right? So when he says it, you gotta believe that he means it. . . . Who else are you going to write to? Have you written to anybody else?" said Carson.

Sam told him that she had written a letter to the queen of England.

Carson looked stunned. "You did? What did you write to Queen Elizabeth about?"

Sam scrunched up her nose. "I just told her I liked her."

"You just said you liked her? What kind of a letter did you get back?" Carson was curious.

"She just said, 'Thanks.'"

"That queen just runs off at the mouth sometimes," Carson said.

He asked Sam what she wanted to be when she grew up.

"Veterinarian," Sam answered.

"What's the most important thing you should do with a dog? If you have a dog."

"Feed him," Sam replied.

"Feed him. That is why I kept losing them. I remember Rover went just like that. Never fed him. No, I am just teasing. Well, you are a delightful young lady. And you are a pretty young lady, too."

Carson then wanted to know whether she'd heard of him.

"They told me you were a comedian."

"And did you believe them?" Carson asked.

"Yes," Sam replied, laughing.

Carson thanked Sam and then kissed her good-bye.

"Heard you were a comedian," he quipped to his sidekick, Ed McMahon, when Sam exited the stage.

"Another one of your great fans," laughed McMahon.

With the interview over, they headed back to the hotel, where Sam and Lynn spent the rest of the day splashing in the pool. The next day Disneyland awaited them.

Back in Manchester, some of Sam's classmates greeted her with "Hey, I saw you on TV!" Others commented that they found her dangling legs hilarious.

"But they never commented if I was any good," she said when she got home from school.

8

MR. MOM

In the spring of 2013, in Jane's sunny dining room in Boothbay, Maine, family pictures are spread across the table. There is one of eighteen-month-old Sam in the winter of 1973—bundled up in a snowsuit, squealing in delight at the amount of snow on their front porch in Amity. In another snapshot, little Sam and her grandmother Nonnie are peeking from under the dining room table where the two had built a fort. And there is seven-year-old Sam on a swing in their Amity backyard, her toes reaching for the sky. I picked up a long, narrow frame with four black-and-white photographs of Arthur and Sam, aged five.

"Those were done when the photo booths just appeared in the malls. Neither one of them knew that it was a series of shots," Jane says.

The first picture shows the two of them smiling at the camera. In the next one, Arthur looks befuddled, his mouth wide open. Sam looks up at him, surprised to see that there is something her daddy doesn't know. By the third click, Arthur has figured out that there is more than one shot, and so he relaxes into another smile, while Sam, unprepared for the shutter, covers her mouth with her hand. The two hadn't known there would be the fourth click, and the camera captured them on their way out, Arthur bending down to pick up a shopping bag and opening a booth curtain, while Sam, pleased as punch, is still sitting on the stool but looking away from the camera.

"I love this photo of them," Jane comments. "It shows how close the two of them were."

Those first days after Andropov's letter arrived, a bit overwhelmed by the unexpected invasion, Arthur and Jane talked about the excessive amount of attention that descended on their household. "Is all of this good for Sam?" they wondered. They tried to anticipate the reporters' questions so that Sam would have time to think about what she might be asked. But Sam seemed unperturbed. "That's OK, I can handle it."

She seemed to be really enjoying herself, and so, for the time being, they decided, they would just roll with it. Later, if for some reason things got more complicated, they could stop the crazy momentum by simply not answering their phone.

But Sam wasn't the only one Jane was concerned about. She was also worried about Arthur.

His first heart attack in the late spring of 1978 in Amity, when Arthur was thirty-eight years old, came as a shock. As chairman of the English Department at Ricker College and the elected faculty representative to the school's board of trustees, Arthur took on extra teaching assignments as the college was trying to stay open amid decreased enrollment and faculty departures. Then their beloved dog Gar got very sick and died in a matter of days. For weeks a cloud of sadness was lifted only occasionally by Sam's antics. Ricker closed two months after Gar's death, leaving Arthur out of a job. They now were relying on Jane's income, which was hard on Arthur, who saw himself as his family's protector. Then, a few weeks later, a flu was going around, and it seemed that Arthur had caught it. It was a strange one that wouldn't let up. One afternoon, he called her at work complaining of pain. At the hospital, the doctor said there was nothing to worry about and sent them home; then he called to tell them that the blood test indicated elevated enzymes. The cardiologist diagnosed a myocardial infarction.

Arthur worked out, was the founder of the weightlifting club at Ricker, competed in shot put, and played lacrosse. He didn't look like a heart attack candidate, but heart trouble ran in his family. His father, Clem, a physician himself, had died after his fifth heart attack at the age of fifty-eight—on Thanksgiving, when Jane and Arthur were visiting him and Arthur's mom Theresa with then six-month-old Sam. And Arthur smoked.

Slowly, Arthur got better and was able to find some part-time teaching work, taking on more household duties since he now spent a lot more time with Sam than Jane did. He took Sam and her little friends shopping and to the movies and listened to their endless chatter during playdates at their house. On his job application for a teaching position that opened up in 1980 at the University of Maine, Augusta, he listed "house-husband" and substitute teacher as his "current occupation."

In the fall of 1980, Jane got her job transferred to Augusta, and on Halloween of 1980, they arrived in Manchester, a small town a few minutes outside Augusta. For a time, their lives returned to a predictable routine: Sam attended Manchester Elementary, Jane settled into her job in Augusta, and Arthur started teaching at the university. He was feeling great and even resumed his shot put training at nearby Maranacook Community School—until one afternoon in April 1981 when he collapsed right there on the school's field. He never lost consciousness, but that heart attack was a big one. He spent days in intensive care, with Jane, Sam, and Theresa in the waiting room, worried that he might not recover.

"Is Daddy going to die?" Sam asked.

After weeks of rest, medications, and tests, the doctors determined that he needed a quintuple bypass surgery, which was performed in August 1982 at the Maine Medical Center in Portland.

He was a sight to behold when they first saw him after the surgery: not allowed to wash for three days, he was rugged and unshaven, but his weak smile made them very happy. Then there was a long recovery. Excruciating pain made it hard for Arthur to walk from the couch to the typewriter and left him completely exhausted even after the smallest task.

"Can I see your scars, Dad?" Sam asked one day. Arthur obliged, revealing the scars on his chest and legs.

"That's gross, Dad!" she said. Five minutes later, she returned, asking to see them again. She measured them all, counting thirty-six inches in total.

In the months after the operation, Jane had finally relaxed, thinking that the worst was over. Albeit slowly, Arthur was getting stronger. He quit smoking. Theresa drove Sam to track meets, helped with their new dog, Kim, and had dinner ready when Jane got back from work.

But then Sam's letter got published in *Pravda*, and their life descended into a flurry of phone calls, interviews, and trips. Arthur was doing his best answering the phone, their kitchen having turned into an impromptu media-briefing hub. He looked like he was having fun, but Jane was worried—all this activity was potentially very stressful.

Reporters and photographers were now congregating in groups in their front yard, kitchen, and living room. Boxes of Sam's crayons shared the coffee table with journalists' notebooks and file folders. Camera bags and microphone wires were strewn all over the living room. There were TV crews from England, Australia, Germany, and Bulgaria. A photographer traveled from Paris to take pictures of the family on their front porch. The Soviets sent their TV crew as well—after receiving special permission to travel to Manchester, which was near the Brunswick Naval Air Station. When the US crews heard that the Soviets were coming to film Sam, they wanted to come film the Soviets filming. With Jane at work all day, it fell to Arthur to coordinate all their comings and goings.

9

04351 TO 163001

MAY 1983, ARKHANGELSK, USSR

I don't remember exactly how I ended up in front of the TV that evening. I might have been working at the folded dining room table that doubled as my desk in the corner of our living room, when Baba Valia started saying, "Seichas, seichas" ("now, now"), faster and more excitedly as she waved her hand trying to get my attention—all the while intently looking at the TV so that she herself didn't miss anything. Since Baba Valia had "discovered" Samantha Smith and introduced her, so to speak, to our family, she felt the responsibility of staying abreast of the developing situation. Her interest inspired my mom. My brother and sister, six and four at the time, didn't share in the excitement—they were most likely occupied with their toys in the bedroom.

Soon the news anchor appeared on my black-and-white TV. "We're guests of Samantha Smith," he said, introducing the special about the Soviet TV crew visiting Samantha and her family in her hometown of Manchester, Maine.

As the camera panned on the intersection, I noted the unfamiliar writing on the white road signs and the different-looking cars. Soon white, two-storied houses appeared, and the narrator talked about Samantha's hometown. "The little town of Manchester, Maine, in the southeastern part of Maine, is so tiny that it is not marked on every map. There are only two or three streets in Manchester and the houses have no numbers. To find the Smith family, we had to visit the local post office."

The camera zoomed in on the "04351" zip code plaque on the one-story Manchester post office.

"And here is Samantha herself, along with her father, Arthur Smith, a university professor in the state capital of Augusta, and her mother, Jane," announced the narrator.

A girl's face appeared on my screen. She looked positively lovely, if a bit shy. She had bright eyes, a slightly upturned nose, and a pretty smile. Standing in a meadow with tall trees behind her, she wore a light-colored turtleneck and jeans. She wiggled quite a bit, and I immediately felt a kinship with her fidgetiness. How many times I'd gotten into trouble when I couldn't stand still at the street corner as my mom finished a conversation with a friend.

The girl's shoulder-length hair was dark, like mine. It was split in the middle and secured with two barrettes. I liked the hairstyle. "I'm growing mine out," I thought to myself.

Not that long before, my hair had also been shoulder length and wavy. I had opted for short layers on the spur of the moment the year before, tired of the ponytails hitting my face during spins on the ice. My mother's attempts at subsequent trims didn't add much to my look. I tried to tame my "sparrow that got stuck in the vacuum cleaner" hairstyle by wrapping a rubber band around a handful of hair at the very top of my head. The shoulder length would look so much better!

Samantha's mom, I noted, looked a lot like mine. Like my mom, Jane was thin and pretty, and her hair was short and curly. At one moment, Jane's hand gently touched Samantha's back to turn her daughter's attention to the camera that was filming them in the yard. She wasn't upset, I could tell; the smile on her face reflected only pride. Jane glanced at Samantha's father, who confidently surveyed the cameras. He was tall and good-looking with kind, soft eyes. He wore a sweater over a checkered shirt. He didn't look like my dad, although my dad was good-looking too. Arthur seemed happy to be with Samantha, and she seemed happy around him.

My parents divorced two months after my fifth birthday in November 1980. A ship navigator with the Arkhangelsk Trading Company, my dad was gone for most of my early years—traveling abroad or around the Soviet Union—and after the divorce he seldom visited. His drinking problem didn't promise much of a future between us.

The camera panned along the white building that was Samantha's school. "Samantha is a typical American schoolgirl. She attends the fifth grade of the local elementary school. American children start school when they turn five," the narrator explained.

I counted how old I would be in the fifth grade; I was sure I would be eleven. It sounded cool to be ten in the fifth grade; yet, somehow, I didn't like the idea of starting school any earlier.

Now inside her house, Samantha paused at the bookshelf. "She likes to read during her free time," the narrator said. "She is a sports enthusiast, she loves roller-skating, and although it is not completely suited for girls, Samantha likes soccer."

Even though I'd never tried roller skates, I could see the attraction. Yet I didn't quite get how a girl could like soccer. Girls didn't play it in the Soviet Union; I mean, we kicked the ball to each other, even on the field sometimes, but boys wouldn't call it soccer. And they were right; I called it "kicking the ball." Figure skating or gymnastics looked so much more elegant than chasing a ball around a field. Did the boys in America not claim soccer as their own sport?

"Still, it is not only sports and school activities that take up Samantha's time," continued the narrator. "Having lived in the atmosphere of continuous war psychosis, anti-Soviet hysteria that is spread in the United States, Samantha, along with other children and adults in America, feels a deep concern about the threat of a nuclear war. Could everything she hears on the daily TV news, the radio, and in the newspapers be true? To get answers to her questions, Samantha wrote to Moscow, to Yuri Vladimirovich Andropov."

Samantha was now sitting on the couch in her living room. The Soviet reporter sitting next to her wore thick tortoiseshell glasses that made him look like a school principal. Yet that didn't seem to faze Samantha. He wanted to know why she had written to Yuri Andropov.

"Well, nuclear war is on a lot on our TVs in America," she said. "I think I know what Mr. Reagan thinks of it. But what does Mr. Andropov think? I decided to write to him and ask him about it."

I could hear bits of her voice in the pauses between the Russian translation, and I wished I could understand what she was saying without the interpreter.

"Did Samantha get the answers to her questions?" asked the correspondent.

"Yes, he answered my questions. Mr. Andropov says that the Soviet Union really doesn't want to conquer the world. I get a lot of letters about it myself these days," Samantha answered.

Her face was really animated; she smiled and scrunched up her nose, and sometimes she cocked her head to one side and her eyebrows shot up. I, too, loved making faces. In my composition for Nina Mikhailovna's Russian class, titled "Who Do I Want to Be When I Grow Up," I wrote that I wanted to be a clown. What am I doing to prepare for my job now? "I put my grandmother's pants on my head and dance around to make my siblings laugh," I wrote. I got only a satisfactory grade and a suggestion to reconsider. Nina Mikhailovna thought a clown was not a good choice of an occupation. I was confused—Baba Valia and I loved watching the Soviet circus programs on TV with their hilarious clowns and graceful acrobats. Having such a job seemed like pure joy.

Samantha's face filled my black-and-white TV screen, and I examined her closely. Americans were supposed to be the enemy, and yet she looked just like me—if I had long hair.

"Are any of your friends afraid of nuclear war?" asked the reporter.

"Many of them. Probably all of them," she answered.

"What do you know about the Soviet Union?"

"Samantha says that she knows very little," the narrator said. "They don't teach much about the Soviet Union at her school," he added. I didn't know much about her country either.

"But I know that the Soviet Union is a beautiful country," said Samantha. I wanted to know how she could be so sure.

"Does Samantha want to come to the Soviet Union at the invitation of Yuri Vladimirovich Andropov?"

"Very much so."

"When?"

"This summer."

Then the Smiths were on their front lawn again, and Sam closed her eyes and giggled at something. I wanted to step into the screen and find out what she was giggling about.

The next shot showed Samantha with her father and another girl. "This must be Samantha's friend," I thought. The girl wore capri pants and was much shorter than Samantha. There now were two normal-looking American girls and a set of parents.

"And of course, it is a sensation," the narrator continued enthusiastically, "but also a reason for evil outbursts. Take the correspondent from the American news company NBC, for example. Once he found out that Samantha would be shown on Soviet TV, he claimed that she would be used for Moscow's propaganda." The camera showed the back of a bushy-haired man with a large camera bag. I didn't know what "propaganda" meant, but I sensed that maybe someone thought the interview was a bad idea. I already liked this girl, so I disagreed.

Samantha and her parents appeared for the last time on the front porch of their house, bidding reporters (and me) farewell.

With the interview over, we all sat around the TV for a little bit longer.

"The town looks really small," Baba Valia noted, "almost like the village I grew up in." Baba Valia left her village at the age of fourteen to go to school and never went back.

"Small, but kind of cute," I thought. While our "Sleeping Skyscraper" looked a lot more imposing, these little white houses looked straight out of a fairy tale. Maybe houses in Baba Valia's village looked like they were from a fairy tale, but I suspected it was a darker one.

I noticed that the trees in Manchester didn't have any leaves yet—just like the trees in Arkhangelsk. But there were also differences. My hometown was larger, much larger—I could see it right away. Arkhangelsk was an important Soviet port and would be celebrating its four hundredth birthday in 1984. My zip code was longer too—it had six digits: 163001. I wrote it at the bottom of the envelopes I sent to a Bulgarian girl named Mariela who became my first foreign pen pal thanks to a project Nina Mikhailovna started with a teacher at a school in Sofia. Mariela was learning Russian in school, but she often used Bulgarian words if she forgot the Russian ones. Since the two languages use the same alphabet, reading her letters was a lot of fun. *Moia maika* meant only one thing in Russian: "my undershirt." In Bulgarian, Nina Mikhailovna explained, it meant "my mother." Realizing that there was more than one way to say things was fascinating.

Our main post office stood next to the sprawling city square: it was five stories high with many tall windows and heavy doors. I had to dig in my heels and pull on the ornate door handles when I attempted to pry those doors open. Most of the time, I needed my mom's help.

I also didn't see any trams in Manchester. Arkhangelsk had many trams that jangled on rails and stretched their giant electric antennas to the overhead wires. It also had buses that didn't use rails or antennas, plus trolley buses that used antennas but no rails. The green tram ticket could be purchased while on board by slipping a three-kopeck coin into the slot and then turning the handle of the heavy ticket machine that hung between the tram windows. Often, a serious-looking conductor walked by with the ticket punch, but on some trams one could validate one's own ticket by sliding it between the two large metal plates of the automatic ticket punch and pressing the handle down. Sometimes old ladies would assume the job of volunteer conductor: "Don't forget to punch your ticket," they'd remind you as soon as it rolled out of the ticket machine.

In his letter, Yuri Andropov called Samantha "courageous" and her question "the most important of those that every thinking man can pose." The fact that the general secretary praised this girl for asking questions puzzled me greatly: asking questions wasn't usually encouraged in the Soviet Union of my childhood. It was especially frowned on in school, as doing so implied that there was something you didn't know, which, of course, was nothing to be proud of. Asking questions of superiors undermined their authority, which was clearly inappropriate. So, yes, in that respect, Samantha was courageous. But maybe something in this girl's upbringing or the place where she was from welcomed this kind of questioning. The more I considered this idea, the more curious I became—even though I still thought it was unfair that the American girl had been invited to Camp Artek.

"Starting school at five years old, huh?" Mom asked.

"That's too early! And way too much work," I said.

"True," Mom agreed.

"And how about soccer?!" I asked. "Did you hear that she plays soccer?!"

"That is amazing," said Baba Valia. "She must be a pistol!"

10

FOUR MINUTES
TO MIDNIGHT

1982–1983, UNITED STATES AND SOVIET UNION

Just as Samantha wanted to know why the Soviets wanted to conquer the world, I wanted to know why Americans were our enemies.

"Because they have nuclear bombs," answered Baba Valia.

I wanted to know whether we had nuclear bombs.

"Yes, but . . . the Soviet Union would never use them. We have them to protect ourselves from them."

"What if the Americans use the nuclear bombs on us," I pressed, "and then we use our bombs on them? What would happen then?"

"There'd be nothing left. Americans used nuclear bombs a long time ago on Hiroshima and Nagasaki in Japan. They leave nothing behind. You just disappear."

"Just like that? Nothing left?"

"Yes, just like that."

I wanted to know why Americans hated the Soviets, but Baba Valia didn't know the answer.

Thirty-some years later, as I read about the Soviet-American relations of the 1980s, I realized that as Samantha's letter made its way to the Kremlin, people on both sides of the ocean had the same question: Did the other nation plan to start a war? It looked like even at the highest levels of government, there were more questions than answers.

57

While 1983 welcomed the fiftieth anniversary of Soviet-American diplomatic relations, the distrust between the two superpowers was at its height. The Americans saw the Communist Soviets as everything that was wrong with the world. The Soviets thought the same of Americans. In 1981, the Bulletin of the Atomic Scientists moved the hand on the proverbial Doomsday Clock to four minutes to midnight. And while the intelligence services on both sides were working overtime, little was known as to the actual threat the other presented. In May 1983, George Kennan, an expert on Soviet-American relations, would declare that the increasingly hateful rhetoric, omnipresent distrust, and "militarization of thought" had "the unfailing characteristics of a march toward war—that, and nothing else."

The Soviet military officials, unable to forget the surprise attack by Hitler's forces in June 1941, clung to the mantra that "1941 shall never be repeated." The utter shock of that summer forty years before, when the German ground and air attacks incapacitated the Soviet forces in just a few hours, guided all Soviet foreign relations decisions. No Soviet citizen wanted to wake up to the shattering news of another invasion; hence they could not afford to be trusting in their relations with the West.

By 1982, no direct communication existed between the leaders of the two superpowers, and neither had a way to understand what the other side might be thinking. In 1982, West German chancellor Helmut Schmidt said to George Shultz, "The superpowers are not in touch with each other's reality. The Soviets can't read you. More human contact is needed." "Relations between the superpowers were not simply bad; they were virtually non-existent," Shultz said of the situation years later. The personal and confidential channel established by Henry Kissinger to work directly with Soviet ambassador Anatoly Dobrynin on the matters of national security was abruptly closed soon after Ronald Reagan's inauguration. When Dobrynin's car pulled up to the back gates of the White House in the first days of Reagan's presidency, it was turned around. Now the only communications each government received as to the other's intentions came via official speeches and news broadcasts.

The ascent of Yuri Andropov, a former KGB chief, to the highest post in the Soviet leadership in November 1982 was met with mixed emotions around the globe. An article in the November 22, 1982, issue of *Time* magazine that Jane had showed to Samantha referred to Andropov as a "closet liberal" who seemingly harbored hopes for the betterment of Soviet-American relations. In Moscow, the assistant director of the International Department of the Communist Party, Anatoly Chernyaev (whose diaries I read at the National Security Archive in 2015), also wondered as to the changes the Andropov era might bring.

A man of formidable intellect, Chernyaev held high hopes for his new boss. He was quick to spot substantial differences in the material published in *Pravda* and other government papers—the typical "nasty bragging" gave way to more critical pieces. He was particularly moved by an exchange he witnessed during Andropov's visit to a Moscow factory. There, Andropov invited the audience for an unexpected Q&A session. An elderly factory worker, heartened by the sudden atmosphere of openness in the auditorium, stood up.

"Yuri Vladimirovich, can I start with something unpleasant?"

"That's what we are here for," Andropov replied.

"Where were you when we needed you?"

After a short pause, Andropov's voice cut through the deathly silence. "Same place as you."

The very idea that all citizens were responsible for where the country ended up was an entirely new concept in the Soviet Union of the early 1980s. It invited the unexpected notion that the country had indeed arrived somewhere it wasn't supposed to be. "May God grant him at least five good years!" Chernyaev wrote in his diary.

My mom's memories of Andropov are permanently associated with the lunchtime raids on movie theaters. So lax was the Soviet work ethic in the 1980s that people would take extended lunch breaks and head over to the cinema for a movie rather than return to work. While my mom found movie theaters a waste of time and money (which was particularly tight after her divorce), she might make an occasional stop at the store after her lunch rather than returning directly to her job—in case some "deficit" item suddenly appeared on the shelves.

In November 1982, when I stood by my living room couch watching Leonid Brezhnev's funeral procession on my black-and-white TV, Vice

President George H. W. Bush was in Moscow as the head of the American delegation. After the funeral, Bush joined US Ambassador Arthur Hartman and Secretary of State George Shultz for a private meeting with Yuri Andropov, as well as the Soviet minister of foreign affairs, Andrei Gromyko (known in the West as "Mr. No"), and Andropov's assistant, Andrey Alexandrov-Agentov.

At that meeting, Bush noted a welcome change from Leonid Brezhnev—after shaking some two thousand hands, Andropov seemed energetic and, in conversation, displayed an admirable intellect. Of course, not much was needed to surpass the lethargic responses of Brezhnev in his last years. Rumor had it that Andropov wasn't well either. The grim state of the new Soviet leader's health was obvious to George Shultz, who said, "He looked more like a cadaver than did the just-interred Brezhnev, but his mental powers filled the room." Andropov reminded Shultz of "Sherlock Holmes's deadly enemy, Professor Moriarty, all brain in a disregarded body." Shultz "put him down as a formidable adversary." In his memo to the deputy director of intelligence, he described Andropov as "ready to take us on."

It is said that the newly elected Reagan was "of two minds" regarding Soviet-American relations, but even those who knew him well couldn't always agree as to which might prevail. While his public rhetoric was strongly anti-Communist, in private Reagan continued to express eagerness for contact with Moscow. On the snowy evening of February 12, 1983, in the wake of one of the harshest blizzards Washington had experienced in the twentieth century, President and Mrs. Reagan cancelled their weekend plans at Camp David and invited Secretary of State Shultz and his wife to dinner instead.

That impromptu dinner is said to have laid the groundwork for the shift in Reagan's attitude toward the Soviets. Having followed Shultz's televised tour of China, the president inquired about making a similar trip to China and the Soviet Union. While the two men discussed the possibilities of the proposal, Reagan confided that some of his staff wouldn't support it. His own rhetoric, he acknowledged, wasn't helping matters either.

Recognizing the potential, Shultz mentioned his upcoming meeting with Ambassador Dobrynin, which was scheduled as part of the comprehensive review of Soviet-American relations.

"What would you think about my bringing Dobrynin over to the White House for a private chat?" he offered.

"Great," Reagan replied. He wanted the meeting to be kept secret. "I don't intend to engage in a detailed exchange with Dobrynin, but I do intend to tell him that if Andropov is willing to do business, so am I."

When, on February 15, Ambassador Dobrynin and his aides arrived at Shultz's seventh-floor office at the State Department, they were informed that President Reagan wanted to see them privately. Dobrynin, a veteran of US-Soviet diplomatic relations who had worked with every president since John F. Kennedy, was surprised but kept his thoughts private. He followed Shultz into a restricted elevator to a basement garage where a car was waiting for them. Once at the White House, under strict security, they were escorted to the family quarters on the second floor.

This secret meeting between the American president and the Soviet ambassador was Reagan's first "substantive conversation" with any senior Soviet representative since taking office three years before. "Probably people in the Soviet Union regard me as a crazy warmonger," Reagan said during the meeting, "but I don't want a war between us, because I know it would bring countless disasters. We should make a fresh start." Reagan proposed reestablishment of the personal and confidential channel with the Soviet leader.

Yet, on March 8 of that same year, not even a month after the secret meeting with Dobrynin, Reagan's anti-Communist rhetoric took center stage at the National Association of Evangelicals in Orlando, Florida. During his speech, Reagan called the Soviet Union "the evil empire," a phrase destined to become a maxim for Reagan's approach to the Soviets. The evangelical convention was not the place anyone expected the president to take a stance on Soviet-American relations, and George Shultz would later comment that neither he nor anyone else outside the White House had a chance to review the proposed speech.

On hearing the speech, Andropov referred to Reagan as insane and a liar. In a private conversation with Dobrynin, he expressed concern. "Is he just playing his game and being a hypocrite, or does he really realize that for all our ideological disagreements, you just cannot bring about a confrontation in the nuclear age?" "We should be vigilant," Andropov continued, "because he is unpredictable. At the same time, we ought not to ignore any signs of his readiness to improve our relations."

11

"SHE NEEDS TO SEE THE ANSWERS FOR HERSELF"

MAY–JUNE 1983, MANCHESTER, MAINE

On May 6, the *Lewiston Daily Sun* announced that the Soviet trip was "in the works for Samantha Smith" and quoted Soviet ambassador Anatoly Dobrynin as saying that the Soviet government had offered the family an all-expenses-paid, two-week tour of Moscow, Leningrad, and Crimea—the area that included the Artek children's camp.

For Sam, there was only one problem with the invitation: Camp Artek. "I don't really like camps that much," she told the reporters in one of the interviews.

She had once gone to a Girl Scout camp and been so homesick that Jane had to pick her up early. When this became news, someone put Jean McMullan, the director of the Alford Lake Camp in Hope, Maine, in touch with Jane. McMullan, a camp enthusiast and a veteran camper herself, had organized her first day camp at age fifteen and was determined to change Sam's mind about camps. Jean invited Sam and her friend Lynn to try out the Alford Lake Camp, an all-girls camp situated on over four hundred acres of hills and woods with many activities to choose from. Jane drove Sam and Lynn to the camp, where they rode horses, canoed, and did archery; to Jane's great relief, by evening of that day, both girls wanted to come back the following summer. There was hope for Camp Artek.

In the meantime, Arthur's collection of news clippings was growing. Political cartoons depicting Sam, signed by the artists, started to arrive in Manchester. Arthur framed each one. One pictured Reagan's advisors George Shultz and Roger Stone looking sheepish as Reagan berated, "Struck out? Both of you? Well, we aren't done yet!" In the insert, Reagan was getting on the phone, asking, "What's the latest word from Samantha Smith?"

Another cartoon showed Reagan and Andropov on opposite sides of a giant round table; Sam sat in the middle with her schoolbooks, milk and cookies, and a puppy at her side. The caption read, "International great powers talks were halted today as the mediator–letter writer, 10-year-old Samantha Smith of Manchester, ME, had to take time off to do her homework."

While there was no official comment from the White House, Samantha's home state's governing bodies had a lot to say about her correspondence with the Soviet leader. US Senator George Mitchell sent her a personal letter from Washington, DC, stating that he was proud to have her as one of his constituents. The members of the Maine State Senate and House of Representatives recognized Samantha on April 27, 1983, for her diplomatic efforts and invited her to visit the Maine State Senate at her convenience. On May 10, Sam, with Jane and Arthur in tow, paid a visit to the Maine State Senate, which had just passed a resolution describing her as "Maine's foreign diplomat." They called her "a beam of sunlight from Manchester" who "sparked a glimmer of hope in the coldness of international relations" and offered her "every best wish and Godspeed on her forthcoming trip to the Soviet Union."

Maine Senate president Gerard P. Conley said in his address, "Even some of the most successful diplomats over the past 30 years have failed to do what she's done. . . . She's even managed to steal more than her share of headlines from Secretary of State Shultz," he noted. On a visit to Governor Joseph Brennan's office, Jane and Arthur proudly looked on as Brennan said, "You've been an inspiration to young and old alike in Maine." Right after the meeting, Sam went back to school for her social sciences class.

When the Soviet embassy asked the Smiths which places they wanted to see in the Soviet Union, they started making a list: Red Square, the Kremlin, the Moscow Circus, the Hermitage. Jane pulled out pictures of her college trip to the Soviet Union. On learning about Lenin's Mausoleum, where the embalmed body of the first leader of the Soviet state was displayed, Sam wanted to see it because she'd "never seen a dead person before." Arthur bought Sam a Russian phrase book, and she practiced the Russian phrases for "hello," "thank you," and "you're welcome."

They hoped that their trip would be "a low-profile, educational experience for Samantha, not a press circus," but the press accompanied them at every step. The reporters were there even when Arthur took Sam shopping for gifts for their Soviet hosts. Since the Soviets were going to promote their country, they decided to promote Maine and bought T-shirts from Colby, Bates, and Bowdoin colleges. They also packed tote bags, posters, books, and pamphlets. They managed to keep only one gift secret from the press, the one they picked out for their high-ranking host, not wanting him to find out what it was before they gave it to him.

Bags of letters arrived daily as well—some praising Sam's diplomatic efforts, others full of criticism, calling her a pawn of Soviet propaganda. There were also letters from Soviet Jewish émigrés in Europe, Israel, and the United States begging Sam to pass their requests for exit visas on to Andropov. The stories of families separated, unable to get exit visas, were heartbreaking to read. One newspaper published an open letter from a girl named Irina Tornopolskaya, who, following Samantha's example, had written to Andropov to get her father, a Soviet scientist, released from jail. "We have already waited four years for permission to leave. Now papa has been arrested and we don't know what will become of us." No response from Andropov followed, reported the paper.

Not knowing any of these people personally, Jane and Arthur faced a real dilemma. As the personal guests of the Soviet government, they knew that carrying the letters wouldn't endear them to their hosts. Not taking the letters didn't seem right either. Finally, on advice from a family friend, they decided to take as many letters as they could and deliver them to the Soviets in private.

Arthur also contacted the State Department to ask about its views on the trip. The State Department was cordial, saying that this was their decision and that "if they decided to go, the Department would assist however possible"—both in the United States and in Moscow. It did warn him that the Soviets were "using and would continue to use the invitation for political and propaganda purposes." Arthur said he was aware of that, adding that he didn't want Samantha's visit to resemble that of Billy Graham, the prominent evangelist who, a year earlier, was heavily criticized for his pandering to the Soviets as he claimed there was no denial of religious freedom in the Soviet Union.

"Samantha isn't as naive," Arthur offered to the State Department official.

The State Department suggested a briefing prior to the trip and agreed to send Tom Simons, director of Soviet affairs in the Bureau for European and Canadian Affairs, to meet with them when he was traveling to the area in June. Arthur and Jane agreed.

Meanwhile, in Washington, DC, US Secretary of State Shultz and Ambassador Dobrynin met once again to discuss the improvement of Soviet-American relations. Shultz bemoaned the Soviets' apparent reluctance to trust Reagan's desire for improved relations. Dobrynin countered that the world was very much of the opinion that Reagan was the most anti-Soviet president of the past twenty years. Shultz thought that the situation wasn't as dangerous as it might appear.

"Things could be worse," noted Dobrynin sarcastically, "and more dangerous too."

Both diplomats saw clearly that there had been "no essential change" in the relations between the two countries. This meeting would soon be followed by another on June 18. Dobrynin was surprised by what he called "the epidemic of diplomacy" but was "nevertheless encouraged by all the activity."

In Moscow, on May 27, 1983, Anatoly Chernyaev's wartime friend shared that his son-in-law, a successful young doctor, had been administering dialysis treatments to Andropov. Andropov's kidneys were failing. This fact was to never be repeated. "Take a look at his signature when you get a chance," the friend suggested. A few days later, Chernyaev examined one of the signed documents on his desk. He drew a shaky line in his diary. "Like this," he captioned it, "only worse."

The dialysis treatments that spring took Andropov out of the spotlight for weeks, but on June 2 he was well enough to meet with former US ambassador Averell Harriman. Harriman, who had negotiated the Lend-Lease program for providing military aid to the Allies during World War II, was visiting the Soviet Union as a private citizen. Yet, in his preliminary meeting with Secretary of State Shultz, he was asked to relate to the Soviets that the American side wanted a more constructive relationship. At the meeting with Harriman, Andropov expressed "a real worry that we could come into conflict through miscalculation." "Then nothing could save mankind," he said. Harriman assured him, "Americans are just as anxious as the Soviets to develop and improve relations."

In late June 1983, as promised, Tom Simons, director for Soviet affairs in the Bureau for European and Canadian Affairs at the State Department, arrived in Manchester. Years later, Jane remembered the visit as warm and helpful. Aware of the political ramifications of their endeavor, they wanted to know how best to react if the Soviets asked them to do something "they didn't feel comfortable about." Simons said the Soviets wouldn't make the trip difficult for them, as doing so could backfire. "They wouldn't do anything to embarrass you," he told them. Jane and Arthur found that notion reassuring.

In June 2020, Tom Simons, aged eighty-two, on the phone from Cambridge, Massachusetts, remembered volunteering for the visit to Maine. He had plans to visit relatives in Bridgton, northwest of Portland, so Manchester wasn't too far out of his way.

"I don't even remember if I asked anybody about it, but I said why don't I visit the family and the little girl because I think I can help her avoid some trouble by not letting herself be used by this tremendous Soviet propaganda apparatus."

Thirty-some years later, Simons remembered the Smiths' Manchester house as "up on stilts on the side of a hill, looking over a meadow and a stream of some kind" and Samantha as "a darling little girl [and] very self-aware." Since the Smiths used to live by the Canadian border,

Simons put them down as "sort of 1960s radicals." He wanted to be "gentle and reassuring," he said, "because they probably had some sort of animus against the government, but I also wanted to help them avoid any easy mistakes when they were over there."

"I wasn't trying to tell them not to go, wasn't trying to tell them what to say." He wanted Samantha "not to stumble into a Soviet propaganda briar patch."

"The one thing I remember advising them on—not to accept memberships in any Soviet organizations," Simons recalled.

From 1975 to 1977, Simons had served as a political officer in the American embassy in Moscow, where his daughter attended a Soviet school. He recounted that her experience in the Soviet school had been wonderful "because she was treated as a little queen." "The school was rigorous, so she had a great educational experience," he said, adding that "the school was also kind of delicate about asking whether she could sing a song to Lenin."

"And I said, 'No, no, that's fine, she could learn the poem and sing the song.'" But when the Soviets asked whether she could join the pioneers (the Communist twist on the Scouts), Simons replied, "No, no, let's not do that." He continued, "But you know it was very correct of them to ask the question. And so anyway, I wanted to spare Samantha a kind of thoughtless acceptance of that."

In the evenings, when there was a brief respite in attention, Jane and Arthur asked each other again and again whether all of this was getting to be too much. It was becoming clear that their trip was a risk for both governments—and both were doing their best to prepare for it. Despite their growing concerns, the conversations always ended in the idea that it would be unfair not to let Sam make the trip. "She needs to see the answers for herself," they decided.

To the reporters, Arthur offered, "Once they get a load of Samantha, the impact will be strong on the American side. She's very capable of standing up and asking bold questions—which she did in the letter and is even more capable of doing in person."

PART II

JOURNEY

MAY 2013, BOOTHBAY, MAINE

By the time Jane and I met again in the spring of 2013, we had exchanged hundreds of emails—and only some of them were about the website or interview requests. She hugged my then fifteen-year-old son and twelve-year-old daughter, saying, "It feels like I know you!" I had just updated the website for the thirtieth anniversary of their trip to the Soviet Union. As Jane clicked through the pages of the new website, she looked up at me and said, "You have enough here to write a book! And you would be a perfect person to do it—you have the perspectives of both sides!" I dismissed the idea with a laugh. After all, I had never written a book before, and the website was already an involved hobby. But I guess she did plant a seed.

That day, I followed her up the stairs to the attic of her house in Boothbay, Maine. It had been years since she sold the two-story house on Worthing Road in Manchester. We planned to look through Samantha's toys to see which ones could be donated to the Samantha Smith Collection at the Maine State Museum. Out of Sam's toy chest, my daughter pulled a tiny brown rabbit that fit perfectly in her hands. Then came a giant grey wolf, a stuffed porcupine, and a wooden dog puppet with large, black permanent marker spots and strings made of fishing line that went up to two crisscrossed sticks.

"Sam made it herself—used a tiny saw and all," Jane said.

It took my daughter only a few seconds to figure out how to operate the toy. Soon the dog walked, lifting its big paws high up in the air, and then it danced. Jane and I smiled.

As we continued through the toys, Jane picked up a large stuffed doll. "I remember her," she said. "I had planted crocuses in our yard in Amity, and one spring day Sam, still a toddler, walked out into the garden, the doll in hand, and started whacking the flowers with the doll. I don't remember why she did that, but I remember this doll."

I wished the memories weren't so fleeting.

12

NORTHERN SUMMER

JUNE 1983, ARKHANGELSK, USSR

Summers in Arkhangelsk were unpredictable. With temperatures in June mostly in the sixties, it could rain one day and be sunny the next. There was only one sure way to tell whether summer had really arrived in Arkhangelsk: by the strong smell of melting asphalt in the air. As the spring slush faded into the past, revealing the multitude of potholes, the city authorities usually started on the annual road improvements. The improvements traditionally started in the center of town, where the administration buildings and the main post office were, and slowly spread south toward the local bazaar—all the while stopping the operation of trams, trolleys, and buses and forcing the residents to walk for several kilometers to the station where the service picked up again. These improvements became a joke among the townspeople. "The roads are torn up—it must be summer!"

Summer also meant no school, no early mornings at the ice rink, and a lot of free time. There was so much of it, in fact, that it took me several days after school ended to come to my senses from the abundance of it. In the mornings, I would wake up to the smell of hot millet—or, if I was lucky, hot oatmeal or buckwheat cereal—and milk. Buttered white bread and a cup of tea would also be waiting for me in the kitchen. With my mom at work and my younger brother and sister already at day care, I would be the only grandchild for Baba Valia to look after in the mornings.

From my stool at the kitchen table, I'd look past the small gas stove and the chubby white fridge into our apartment yard. Across the road stood a *dereviashka*, an ochre ramshackle of a communal apartment building, its lace-curtained windows the only glamorous thing about it. Next to the *dereviashka* stood our building's only sandbox, the blue wooden square of it beckoning me to come down. In the morning, the yard was empty and quiet. Looking over the roof of the *dereviashka* and through the tall poplars and delicate birch trees, I could see the silver bits and pieces of the Dvina River, but it was still too cold to swim.

I would eat slowly, working around the edges of the bowl first. "You can blow and blow to cool it off," Baba Valia taught me when I was very little, "but if you work around the edges first, you are already eating, and you'll be done sooner." Baba Valia was always full of good advice. Don't waste time. And although it was summer, and I had nowhere to hurry off to, the advice still made sense.

After breakfast, it was time to watch cartoons in the living room. The black-and-white TV once had a working channel dial, but since it had cracked years before and only a metal rod stuck out of its side, I used pliers to switch between the two available government channels. *Nu Pogodi* (You just wait) was my favorite cartoon series about a big dumb wolf and a tricky little rabbit. Its catchy songs and chases amused me to no end.

As I watched the rabbit outrun the wolf once again, I'd check the window to see whether any kids were out yet. After a while, tired of my jumping up and down from the couch and running to the window, Baba Valia would urge, "Maybe you should just go out by yourself, and then someone might see you out of their window and come out to play. Just make sure you brush your hair first. And don't forget the cardigan!"

Fixing my hair into a palm tree style at the top of my head, I pulled on a cardigan and sprinted out the door. The quickest way down was usually the railing, and I could expertly ride it from my third-floor landing all the way down to the first floor without touching the stairs once—slowing down only on the turns.

Once outside, I'd pass under the dainty canopy of the tall birch tree and run past the purple spray of bluebells that were carefully tended by our stout neighbor, a lady named Avgusta. I would head across the small road toward the *dereviashka* to my favorite spot: the "motorcycle tree." An old poplar with two branches broken off just right to form the handlebars, the "motorcycle tree" allowed a child without a bicycle to pretend he or she had one. Later in the day, the line to sit on it might be three or four kids long. Now it stood alone and proud and was all mine to ride. A jump, a few steps up the tree trunk, and I was in the seat. "Vee-zhooz, vee-zhooz!" Leaning in at the turns, I'd drive my motorcycle down a pretend mountain road, going somewhere far away.

From my vantage point, I could see the yard slowly waking up. The boys would come out first, usually heading to the old woodsheds by entrance number 3—chasing each other in a game of cops and robbers. When the more sedate girls emerged, usually carrying a jump rope or a wad of crumpled elastic, I knew it was time to get off my perch. *Rezinochka* (also known as "Chinese jump rope" or "rubber-band skipping") was our favorite game. Made from about three meters of elastic—the kind that went into waistbands—knotted into a loop, the *rezinochka* was just that: a giant rubber band. We'd stretch it until it was taut, and the "it" girl would then "do tricks"—jump inside and over the rubber band, sometimes twisting it around her feet, untwisting it in midair, and landing on top of it. To increase the difficulty of the tricks, we'd move the elastic up from ankle height to the knees and then to the armpits for levels one through six. If the "it" girl missed a trick, the next girl got her turn. If there were more of us and only one *rezinochka*, we'd pair up and get a chance for a do-over.

Rezinochka could occupy us for several hours: we'd all reach level five (and some of us six) many times before lunch. By 1:00 p.m., the apartment windows would open one by one, and those of us who had grandmas would hear their names broadcast from the kitchen windows: "Lena, lunch time!" "Sasha, time to come in!" Those who were home alone during the day would run off on their own as the yard rapidly cleared.

If there was an afternoon kids' movie on TV, we'd stay in for a while to watch it after lunch. A bit after 4:00 p.m., our elderly neighbors would be sitting on the benches by the entrance knitting, reading newspapers, or "gossiping," as Baba Valia characterized their loud commentary on the life of our block. Soon thereafter, our yard once again would turn into a noisy whirlwind of activity. The boys would run up and down the stairs of the old woodsheds by entrance number 3, the girls would fill the air with giggles, and the neighborhood toddlers, back from the day care, would show off their sandcastles to their mothers or grandmas sitting on the blue sandbox's edge.

Still later in the evening, whose arrival in the white summer nights of my hometown could be established only by the slight yellowing of the sky, one could hear the loud shouts from each apartment's window again: "Lena, ti-i-ime to come home!" "Sasha, ho-ome, I said!" Then the silence would descend on our yard, and the night would fall, which was never actually night, as during the summer in Arkhangelsk there was no darkness.

13

ON OUR WAY

JULY 1983, SOVIET UNION

At the beginning of July in 1983, just as Samantha and her family were finishing up their preparations for the trip to Moscow, my suitcase was packed, and I was ready to go to my first pioneer camp. The night before my departure, I had a nightmare about leaving my shoes behind and was happy to wake up in my bed, still in Arkhangelsk, with an opportunity to correct the mistake. In the afternoon, before heading to the train station, my whole family did the traditional "sit for the road" ritual, which required the traveler to sit on his or her suitcase—for good luck. Baba Valia told me to sit on one side of my suitcase, while she balanced on the other side, and my little sister and brother sat on my mom's lap on a bench in the entryway. Even though I didn't quite understand the tradition—the road and sitting didn't quite fit together—I followed the grown-ups' example: after all, a three-day train trip was serious business, and I wanted to make sure I started off right.

At the crowded train station, I followed my mom as she found the correct train and squad number 5, which I was to join. The camp squad system worked its way up from number 5, which was for the youngest kids, aged seven to eight, to number 1 for thirteen- to fifteen-year-olds. I looked around to see those whom I'd be spending the next forty-five days with and breathed a sigh of relief when I saw other kids who looked just as worried as I was.

This was my second trip away from home by myself. When I was five, I had traveled with my preschool class to a retreat in the Soviet republic of Moldavia. I was told it wasn't a "real camp" because I knew everyone in the group, and in "real camps" one had to make friends along the way. My memories of that trip to Moldavia are scarce: I remember the white hats we wore to keep out the sun as we marched to the beach; I used mine to catch bees one afternoon as I sat among the tall flowers in the retreat's garden. The teachers, who found me there, were surprised that I hadn't gotten stung and nicknamed me the "bee tamer." The only photograph from that summer captures me and a friend posing with toys in front of a brick building of the retreat, me holding a ball, coveting my friend's colorful stuffed clown but smiling nevertheless.

On the way to Camp Gaidarovets, my squad took up almost the entire train car. As campers, we rode *platzkart*, or third class. The berths inside the *platzkart* were arranged in groupings of "four plus two": four berths, two top and two bottom, faced each other inside a main cabin, with the two additional berths (also top and bottom) separated from the main cabin by a narrow aisle. There were no doors between cabins, and one could see all the way down the long train aisle; hence everyone had to be creative when getting ready for bed. A sheet tucked under a suitcase on the luggage shelf above served as a good curtain. On my mom's advice, I chose the top bunk across the aisle from the main cabin: if the kids in my cabin weren't particularly nice, I'd have a choice of two more cabins, occupants of which I could easily see, hear, and wave at if necessary. At either end of the train car there was a bathroom. At the head of the car, there was a small private cabin with a noisy sliding door that housed the conductor, known as the *provodnik*, who checked our tickets and made sure that we were on our best behavior. The *provodnik* was also in charge of the giant vat of boiling water for tea that would be served on request in the evenings.

That first night on the train to Camp Gaidarovets, I was cold and sad, wishing I hadn't gone and missing Mom and Baba Valia, but by day two I had slowly eased into the company of my new playmates. We changed trains in a town named Vologda and then in Moscow, where we had a daylong layover and got to see the capital. In the Moscow subway I went on the escalator all by myself and then saw the biggest department store, called TsUM. I had no money to spend, and everybody seemed in a hurry around me. I was mostly in a hurry too, afraid of getting separated from the group. I wanted to make a memory of Moscow, as this was my first time in the capital, but we didn't see Red Square or Lenin's Mausoleum: I suspected that TsUM was chosen for the benefit of our teachers and camp counselors. Hence, of that first trip to Moscow I remember only the fear of getting lost. I realized then that knowing my address wouldn't do me any good and getting back home from Moscow would be a long journey that I wasn't sure I could make all by myself.

Back on the train, I exhaled. As we got farther south, the train got warmer. During the day, we played cards, sang, and told jokes; when tired from it all, we climbed on the top bunks and got dizzy as we tried to count the trees out the window. We walked to the restaurant car for breakfast, lunch, and dinner, jumping over the rattling springs that connected the train cars. Although the springs were covered in rubber, they made a deafening noise, and I was sure I would fall right through them on my first trip to the restaurant car. Soon enough, though, I learned to swing over the springs as I reached out and grabbed the railings of the next car. By day three, the smell of burning rubber mixed with diesel signaled the happy approach of a meal.

Once the train arrived at the destination, I carried my suitcase to the bus. The full-size suitcase was heavy, and I was thirsty, but we all had to carry our own luggage. When the bus arrived at the large sign that read *Gaidarovets*, we got off, and I picked up my suitcase again to carry it to a brick building that served as a boarding school during the school year and in the summer was converted into sleeping quarters for the pioneer camp. The teachers counted us, sent the boys to one wing, and told us girls our room numbers. In our assigned rooms, we rushed to pick our beds, each of us surprisingly getting one without much fighting. I slid my suitcase under my bed, thus signifying the start of my first summer in a real pioneer camp, the first of many more to come.

Meanwhile, in Maine, on July 7, 1983, before heading to the Augusta airport, Arthur, Jane, and Sam posed for a family picture on their front porch with Nonnie and Cousin Tyler, there to take care of the family dog, Kim.

"I'm excited, I guess," Sam said to the reporters at the airport.

Since there were no direct flights from the United States to the Soviet Union, they first flew to Boston and then to Montreal, where they would catch their Aeroflot flight to Moscow. In Boston, reporters were waiting, and so they stopped for a brief news conference. Jane said, "What Samantha's letter has done and what we hope to achieve on our trip is to remind everyone of the importance of freeing all of our children from the threat of nuclear war."

"Do you think you will meet Andropov?" one reporter asked them.

Arthur said they hoped to—if his schedule permitted. When asked about the entreaties Sam had received from Soviet Jews seeking help with exit visas, Arthur replied, "At this point we're unsure what to do with these appeals because Samantha's position as a guest is something we have to consider. Some of these persons seem to think Samantha may have some influence with Soviet leadership. She does not."

At Montreal-Dorval International Airport, a sea of reporters awaited them. So many cameras and microphones were being thrust at them that at one point Sam accidently bit one of the microphones. The Royal Canadian Mounted Police were summoned to escort them outside and into the car provided by the Soviet consulate for their tour of Montreal. During the four-hour layover, they visited the mayor, the botanical garden, the Olympic stadium, and the Soviet consulate. At a press conference at the Montreal-Mirabel International Airport, the reporters were impressed with Samantha's poise. Wrote the *Montreal Gazette*, "And the fresh-faced girl from small-town America showed the press she could handle the tough questions with ease. Asked about a mysterious present she is taking to Andropov, the Grade Five pupil from Manchester, ME . . . refused to say. 'You reporters can't keep a secret,' she replied calmly, looking into the battery of microphones and television lights."

When asked to describe her feelings about "flying halfway around the world to meet Andropov, seeing her name in the papers and on TV," Samantha didn't waste words. "It's fun," she said. It was also reported that the Soviet Union was footing the $10,200 bill for the Smiths' airfare and the two-week trip.

Then it was time for the thirteen-hour Aeroflot flight to Moscow in first class, which they had all to themselves. John Dougherty, a Maine reporter with WCSH (an NBC affiliate), and his crew were on the flight as well. Barbara Quill and her crew from Maine's WGAN (a CBS affiliate) weren't as lucky. The Soviets, not understanding that US TV stations were separate entities, had decided that one crew from Maine was enough and denied their visas. It would take a couple more days and a call from Senator William Cohen to get Quill and her crew to Moscow.

In Sheremetyevo-2, Moscow's international terminal, a dignitary's welcome awaited them. As soon as she stepped off the plane, Sam was greeted with flowers and welcomed by the deputy chairman of the Union of the Soviet Friendship Society, Gennady Yanaev. Another Gennady, this one by the last name of Fedosov, would be taking care of them for the duration of their journey. Fedosov oversaw the America/Canada Department of the Union of the Soviet Friendship Society. Natalia Batova, secretary of the USSR-USA Society, would become Sam's interpreter and constant companion.

As they made their way down the airport terminal, Jane glanced at Sam, who had a look of total disbelief on her face. Serious-looking adults dressed in suits were following her and helping carry her luggage, while the cameras clicked incessantly. In the airport lobby, a group of boys and girls dressed in the Soviet pioneer outfits brought her more flowers, and Sam paused for an interview when a crowd of reporters gathered around. When asked what she would say if she did get to meet Andropov, Sam replied, "He promised me he wouldn't start a war. Americans say they won't start a war either. Then how come we keep making bombs for war if there is no one to start it?" She looked straight at the reporters.

When the reporters asked Jane for her opinion, she commented only that her daughter was a "good example of American youth and it will be good for Russians to get to meet her."

"Both East and West will enjoy good publicity from the visit," finished Arthur. At that first brief press conference, Sam tried her first Russian words: *zdravstvuite* (hello) and *spasiba* (thank you).

Once out of the airport, they got into the black Chaika limousine, which would become their main mode of transportation. The yellow-and-blue Soviet police car escorted their motorcade to the Sovetskaya Hotel, a place reserved for them as special guests of the Soviet government. In their deluxe room, a large dining table was laden with sweets, cheeses, and cakes. Sam, too excited to sleep on their arrival, rode the hotel elevators, even though Jane and Arthur tried to encourage her to take a nap. That evening they had their first official engagement: a trip to the State Central Academic Puppet Theater. The play that night was about two kings upset over a mountain that separated two kingdoms, so they knocked it down. "It was not lost on a little girl from Manchester, ME," noted the reporters in the next day's telecast.

In June 2018, Maine greeted me with a drizzle—much as Arkhangelsk would have, had I gone there instead that summer. I had come for just a couple of days to do some research at the Maine State Museum in Augusta. By then, I had been working on the book for three years. As I climbed the hill from the museum's parking lot, I stopped by Samantha's statue.

"Hey, kid!" I said before realizing that I was now older than Jane was when she took her daughter to the Soviet Union.

In the office, the museum's collections manager, Natalie Liberace, set a box of slides in front of me. They were the ones Arthur had taken on their trip thirty-five years before. Carefully, I put the slides on the viewer and watched their trip unfold before my eyes.

There are the three of them on their front porch on the morning of their departure for Moscow, looking very dapper—Jane in a jacket with a polka-dot dress, Arthur in a blazer and freshly pressed khakis, Sam in a bright yellow sweater, a polo shirt, lilac-colored pants, and sneakers. Then they are at the airport, saying good-bye to Nonnie and friends. There is a shot of smiling Sam visiting the cockpit of their plane to Moscow and one of her on the night of their arrival in Moscow trying out the red rotary phone in their lavish room at the Sovetskaya. Next slide, and there is Sam, laughing and kidding around in the early hours on their first morning in the Soviet Union. Still jet-lagged, Arthur and Sam must have woken up before the reporters and gone for a stroll around the hotel. The streets around them are completely devoid of crowds. In one shot, Sam poses, smiling, by the slogan "We Shall Arrive at the Victory of the Communist Labor"; in the next, she jumps high into the air in a karate move and then immediately assumes an innocent pose in the next shot—just as a Soviet military officer crosses in front of the camera.

After breakfast, the Chaika limousine was back at precisely 9:00 a.m. to take them to Red Square. With their security detail and the interpreters in tow, Jane, Arthur, and Sam walked the thirty yards across the cobble-stoned square and placed a large basket of red gladiolas at the Tomb of the Unknown Soldier, where the eternal flame commemorated the Soviet lives lost in World War II. At Lenin's Mausoleum, which usually had long lines of Soviet citizens queuing to see the founder of their Communist state, the Smiths, as the personal guests of the Soviet leader, were spared the wait. The mood inside the dark mausoleum was solemn, and Jane noticed that Sam, who had initially looked forward to this particular stop on their itinerary, was spooked and couldn't wait to get out.

They paid a visit to the seat of the Soviet government, where the tour guide let Sam sit at the officials' desks, and then to Lenin's office in the Kremlin and the basilicas nearby. Jane was impressed by how mature Sam acted on that first day. Cameras were everywhere, following her every move, her every reaction. She smiled, waved, and shook hands as if this were something she did every day. In the evening, they watched the Soviet coverage of the trip on the TV in their hotel room. The back page of the Soviet newspaper *Izvestia* that week featured a photograph of their arrival at the Sheremetyevo airport.

On their last day in Moscow, Arthur finally decided to give the letters from the Soviet émigrés to Gennady Fedosov, the career diplomat, who met them at the airport and accompanied them at every event. Arthur reckoned he might know the best course of action for the letters. Gennady wasn't happy when Arthur handed him the letters. He now had to figure out the next step and seemed fearful that they might go public with this unplanned part of their trip. Arthur never learned whether the letters got to any higher-ups, but he felt good that he could do at least that much. Neither Arthur nor Gennady mentioned the letters again.

14

THE LEMONY SCENT
OF CYPRESS

JULY 1983, CAMP ARTEK, USSR

During my first week at Camp Gaidarovets, I was puzzled by the dark nights. Early darkness in Arkhangelsk was indicative of winter, but in Gaidarovets, so far south, it was so hot that I knew we weren't anywhere near fall, let alone winter. During white summer nights in my hometown, the skies never got dark, but at Camp Gaidarovets, it got dark by 8:00 p.m. I decided to broach the topic with my camp counselor.

"Why does it get so dark here at night?" I asked.

"Have you fallen off the moon?" she asked.

"Nope," I answered, sensing that she was mocking me, "but where I'm from, there is no night in the summer, and this is just weird!"

"Where are you from exactly?" she insisted.

"Arkhangelsk," I said.

The weekend trips to the beach were the best part of that first summer at the pioneer camp: an entire day of soaking up the sun and splashing in the Azov Sea, followed by ice cream or watermelon as we got back on the bus to head back to camp that evening. We'd scream some of the lyrics to the camp songs and enjoy the summer breeze that blew in the open windows as the bus sped to camp and a hot dinner. By the next morning, we'd be sore from sunburn, and some campers were so red that they had to see a nurse. The rest of us stood up on our beds comparing tan lines and making plans for the next weekend.

On "mail day," our teachers brought in a stack of envelopes from the post office and shouted out our names. I got a letter almost every time—my mom must have known how disappointing it was not to get one on mail day. Her letters were always long and detailed the weather ("still chilly" or "a bit of sun today, we might go to the river") and life in our neighborhood ("nothing new here" or "so-and-so went on vacation, will be back in two weeks"). She also encouraged me to use every opportunity to fatten up ("eat up on that southern summer fruit") and get a proper suntan ("so it lasts till winter"). She also included Baba Valia's updates on Samantha Smith's trip. Baba Valia promised to save all the newspaper clippings for me for the month and a half that I was gone. "She said to tell you that Samantha will be at the Black Sea soon."

The Azov Sea, where I swam, was just north of the Black Sea. "Was that sea really black?" I wondered of its luscious name. Whom would Samantha meet there? Who would be her friends?

The slides at the Maine State Library and Museum captured the Soviet Union of my childhood through the eyes of Arthur, Jane, and Samantha. Thirty-some years after Samantha's journey there, I wanted to see her trip through the eyes of those Soviet adults and children who were lucky enough to spend some of those two weeks in her company.

Locating Natasha Kashirina, a girl who became known as Samantha Smith's Soviet friend, wasn't easy. Jane had lost contact with her, and no one else seemed to have any information. Then, in 2012, for what would have been Samantha's fortieth birthday, Russian TV aired an interview with Natasha, who, it was reported, now lived in Los Angeles. I tried the usual Google and Facebook, but they didn't bring up any tangible leads. Another three years went by, and in 2015, as I watched that interview again, I noticed a vaguely familiar logo. A search through my Outlook inbox revealed an inquiry from a New York–based producer for a Russian channel whom I'd corresponded with a year earlier. I emailed to ask whether she knew the reporter who'd done the 2012 interview. A few days later, I had scheduled an interview with Natasha.

When my Skype window opened, I was surprised to see that, except for a shorter haircut, Natasha didn't look much different from the lively girl next to Samantha in the newspapers I'd seen as a child. It was almost as if she hadn't aged at all!

But it was the story that Natasha told me from her California home that surprised me most of all.

Natasha Kashirina, a sixth grader from Leningrad, planned to spend the summer of 1983 at a pioneer camp; Artek was not in the cards. Not that summer—not ever, really. Then a phone call to her mom changed everything.

The call from Natasha's principal was not out of the ordinary, because Natasha's mother taught English at the same school. The principal had received a *goriashaya putevka*, a last-minute offer that you either use or lose. Someone had just backed out of the trip to Camp Artek, and they needed to find a replacement quickly. "Would you like to send your daughter for a month to Artek?" the principal asked.

Natasha's mother didn't hesitate. "Sure," she replied.

Soon thirteen-year-old Natasha Kashirina, along with other Artek-bound kids from Leningrad, was on the train to Simferopol in Crimea—for the summer of every Soviet child's dreams.

The train trip to Crimea took two days. At first, Natasha tried to keep track of the station names as the train pulled in and out of flat-roofed terminals crowded with passengers getting on or off. But soon she lost track. At each station, the local salesladies walked through the train shouting out the names of pastries they had on their large trays, and sometimes she and her new friends bought some. As the train got farther south, the kids pulled on the heavy handles that unlocked the train windows to let some fresh air in. Natasha climbed on the top bunk, and, letting the wind blow her hair, she imagined what a summer in Artek might be like.

Going to Artek, the "Kingdom of Childhood" (as it was known among the Soviet kids), was a rare opportunity. Natasha wasn't a typical candidate for it—she knew that. She did attend a specialized English school, where she had been learning English since the second grade, and then a music school at the Leningrad Pioneer Palace, where she headed right after school. But Natasha was only a "solid B student" by the time she finished sixth grade—not a high achiever, by any means.

Nor was she particularly well connected. As the only child of an engineer and an English teacher, she lived in a 387-square-foot room in a communal apartment on the corner of S'ezdovskaya Liniya and Repin Streets, where her family shared a kitchen and a bathroom with seven other families. In the years before the October Revolution of 1917, the entire floor had belonged to a single family, but right after the revolution, it housed twenty-five families to one kitchen. The current number of seven families, she was told, was a significant improvement. In their one-room apartment, her father put up a T-shaped divider, providing a separate sleeping area for Natasha, a room of sorts for her parents, and a common sitting area up by the entry door.

When the train arrived at its destination in Simferopol, Natasha climbed onto the bus for the hour-long drive to camp. The bus windows were open, and the air rushing in was balmy and smelled invitingly of lemon or pine—she couldn't tell which. She later learned it was the scent of the cypress trees that were abundant in Artek. She saw the rugged mountains and the azure waters of the Black Sea in the distance. She sensed this summer was going to be one of a kind.

Soon, a tall concrete flame and then a large sign that spelled out "ARTEK" came into view. When they got off the bus, every camper was assigned to one of Artek's ten smaller camps: Morskoi (Sea), Lazurny (Azure), Kiparisny (Cypress), Almazny (Diamond), Khrustalny (Crystal), Yantarny (Amber), Lesnoy (Forest), Ozerniy (Lake), Polevoy (Field), and Rechnoy (River). These camps had their own schedules and programs focusing on leadership, science, arts, crafts, sports, and other outdoor activities. Within those camps, children were assigned to different dorms, or houses, that ranged from contemporary-style cabins to large multistory buildings, which on the outside resembled hotels or university dorms but had up to ten beds in each room. Each camp session lasted thirty days. Thanks to Crimea's agreeable climate, Artek was a year-round camp. In the winter, which was also mild in Artek, campers could attend school on the camp's grounds.

Natasha was to join a troop of over thirty campers within the Sea Camp, which was located right on the Black Sea shore.

Every morning, Natasha woke up to the sound of waves crashing on the beach right outside her window. After the bugle call, there was a morning swim and then breakfast. Although the activities were like those she was accustomed to in other pioneer camps, she soon learned that in Artek everything was taken to the next level. The usual camp hikes in Artek went through the wooded trails of Ayu-Dag, also known as "Bear Mountain," which towered over the camp and was the subject of many local legends. The Artek campers took field trips to nearby Yalta's art and history museums. Camp songs and skits were turned into colorful carnivals with costumes and fireworks, and camp games were led by the most energetic camp counselors she'd ever met. Their daily activities kept them very busy, so when it was time for Artek's traditional quiet time, known as the *absolut* (as it was to be observed with absolute silence and preferably sleep), Natasha didn't mind at all. The afternoon was full of new discoveries, and at night there were giant campfires with songs and more games.

As Natasha made friends, she soon concluded that, contrary to the popular notion that only children of highly placed government officials with extensive connections went to Artek, in fact most of the kids there really deserved to be in this prestigious establishment. Some were active in science clubs in their schools; others were artists, pianists, talented dancers, or aspiring Olympic athletes. There were times when, listening to their debates, Natasha felt inadequate. "What am I doing here?" she asked herself. To be sure, there were kids of "connected" parents who arrived in camp in imported clothes, but this discrepancy was quickly fixed by the requirement to wear the camp uniform: a white shirt, a turquoise skirt for girls or shorts for boys, and a turquoise flight cap to match.

One day, as the summer session was nearing its close, Natasha and her Sea Camp mates were called for an "important meeting" with the camp's director.

"The personal guest of the Soviet leader is coming to Artek," the director announced. "Her name is Samantha Smith, she is eleven years old, and she will be visiting our camp for the last four days of the session!"

The kids were surprised at the announcement. "How can an eleven-year-old be a *personal guest* of the Soviet leader?!" Some had heard of the letter this girl had written to Yuri Andropov earlier that year. Natasha didn't remember hearing about it, but everyone's excitement soon became hers.

"She will be staying in your troop," the director said, turning to the inhabitants of the Sea Camp's Blue House, where Natasha lived—one of the newer dorms in Artek. The girls were excited: an American would be staying in their dorm!

None of them had ever met an American before. Some, like Natasha, had seen foreign tourists on the streets of their hometowns. The tourists' bright outfits stood out in the crowd. During the school year, tourists would sometimes visit the Club of International Friendship at Natasha's school, and she'd see them pass out pencils to the kids in the hallways. There were also meet-and-greet events at the club, when the tourists sat at long tables and answered questions the older students carefully con-structed in advance in English. As a sixth grader, Natasha couldn't yet speak at those meet-and-greets, but when she was invited to listen in, she tried to work out the meaning of the English sentences and imagined what it would be like to ask her own questions someday.

Soon the schedule of the American girl's visit was put together, and Natasha's dorm was scrubbed in preparation for the distinguished visitor. Twelve campers were chosen to meet Samantha and her parents at the Simferopol airport. The director wanted someone who spoke English to greet Samantha. A couple of girls in Natasha's troop spoke some English. Natasha had studied English for five years by then, longer than most of the other campers. She could read it but had never spoken to a foreigner and wasn't sure whether she could even talk to the American girl. Yet, along with the other girls, she worked on memorizing the English speech constructed by one of the camp counselors. Natasha practiced the lines over and over: "Dear Samantha! We wish to welcome you to our country and our camp Artek." On the day they recited the speech in front of the director, Natasha didn't forget any words and was told that she would be the one delivering it.

Other things needed attention as well. The kids greeting Samantha had to look respectable, so Natasha's camp uniform was altered to fit her better. Then someone brought in an iron. Natasha hadn't seen an iron for the entire month she'd spent in camp. Everyone's skirts, shorts, and shirts were ironed. Their red silk pioneer ties were ironed, as were their camp caps, which weren't even wrinkled to begin with. When everything was done, Natasha couldn't recognize herself in the mirror. Her usually wavy hair, now in two tight, long braids, was tied with giant white bows. "Is this really me?" she wondered as she looked at herself in the mirror.

In the summer of 1983, we, the Soviet kids, were sure that Natasha Kashirina had been especially picked to accompany Samantha. Thirty-three years later, I told Natasha that everyone thought she was one lucky girl.

"I don't think anyone anticipated any of this in advance," she replied. "If anybody had done any research on my family, I'd be the last one to be picked. They were not members of the Communist Party, we lived in a communal apartment. . . . [W]e weren't good candidates for an international friend. . . . But by the time they realized who they'd picked, it was too late to check references."

It turned out that, by some act of providence, the girl who became Samantha's best friend in the Soviet Union was just an ordinary Soviet girl—like me.

As Saturday evening and the special guest's arrival drew close, Natasha and the other campers, bouquets in hand, along with the counselors and the camp's accordion player, got into the minivan bound for the Simferopol airport. On the way, their imaginations ran wild.

"Will she be all rich and fancy, just like the other foreigners?" they wondered.

"Is she going to be friendly or stuck up?"

"Will she want to live with us in the dorm?"

"Is her mom going to live with us too?"

At the airport, a crowd of journalists and cameramen was waiting. There were so many of them that Natasha could hardly see the plane.

"Will I be able to give my speech? Will they let me give it?" She was getting worried.

They were led to the front of the crowd, where they took their places, holding the flowers. The boys lined up behind the girls. Then the plane door opened, and a smiling, pretty girl came bounding down the stairs.

Natasha heard one of the boys behind her sigh in astonished relief. "She looks just like any other girl I know!"

Photographers' cameras went into overdrive, and reporters surrounded Samantha and her parents. Patiently Natasha and her friends waited. When the crowd of reporters parted, they saw the girl walk toward them. Natasha took a few steps forward and handed Samantha the bouquet of flowers. She paused for a moment and then decided it was time to start her speech.

"Dear Samantha! We wish to welcome you to our country and our camp Artek. That's why we invite you to our pioneer detachment. We swim, play games and hold our interesting pioneer affairs together. Welcome to our pioneer detachment, dear Samantha!"

"*Spasiba*, thank you," said Samantha; then she smiled shyly and looked around. As if on cue, the other girls rushed up and loaded her with more bouquets.

Back in the minivan, all their earlier worries dissipated in the whirlwind of excitement as they tried to talk to the American girl. Natasha noticed that the smile never left the girl's face, not even for a moment. Samantha looked around the minivan and smiled; she waved to her parents as they were getting their luggage and smiled; she even seemed to know some of the reporters, to whom she waved and smiled.

On their way to camp, the accordion player's fingers hurried up and down the keys as they sang "May There Always Be Sunshine." To Natasha's surprise, Samantha knew the lyrics in English. The boys took it upon themselves to teach her how to sing it in Russian: "Pust vseeg-da boo-det soln-tse!" Samantha seemed eager to learn.

"Chor-no-ye Mor-re!" one of the boys said, pointing out the window when the song was finished. "Black Sea," interpreted Natasha, pointing out the window as well.

Although Natasha spoke more English than Samantha spoke Russian, she quickly realized that the English she learned in school wasn't the English Samantha spoke. She could hardly understand what Samantha was saying. Yet this issue didn't seem to bother Samantha, who quickly resorted to using her hands and face to communicate. And she was good at it, too: her eyes widened, her eyebrows went up, and her hands drew circles in the air. Sometimes she'd cover her mouth in a gesture of subtle embarrassment, as if to signal, "OK, I'll have to start over." The campers quickly caught on to this method of communication, and soon everyone was making faces, with Natasha rarely needing to insert a word here or there. By the time the minivan arrived at Artek, Natasha had decided that this girl could talk to anyone even if she didn't speak their language. They wouldn't have any trouble communicating.

When they entered Artek's stadium, the announcer's voice boomed in Russian, "Samanta Smit!"

The stadium was full of children, all dressed in camp uniforms, red ties a-blazing, chanting her name in Russian. "Sa-man-ta! Sa-man-ta!" There were over a thousand children there—the entire Sea Camp was present and accounted for! Some were holding balloons and large welcome banners. "We are glad to meet you in our Artek," the banners proclaimed in both English and Russian. "May there always be sunshine!" "May the children always laugh!" declared others. Everyone was chanting Samantha's name and clapping.

Then a beautiful Russian folk song came over the loudspeakers, and six girls dressed in Russian national costumes slowly made their way toward Samantha from the other end of the stadium. As they drew nearer, they moved back one by one in an intricate, almost balletic routine, and then a girl and a boy emerged from their midst. They were carrying bread and salt on an ornate towel, the traditional Russian greeting of a dear guest.

Samantha, by now standing alone by the microphone with an armful of flowers and her little beige purse over her arm, was so surprised, she was speechless. The girl in the national costume handed Samantha the bread and salt, which Samantha accepted. Not knowing what to do with them, she looked around. "They probably don't have a bread-and-salt greeting in America," Natasha thought. Samantha looked so small and lost out there by herself that Natasha gingerly moved past her fellow campers and came to her new friend's rescue, showing how the greeting is properly accepted. "Like this"—Natasha made a gesture of breaking the bread and dipping it into the salt—"and then eat."

The girl and boy in folk costumes bowed before Samantha, almost touching the ground with their hands, and moved back as the melody came to an end.

Then it was time for Natasha to give her speech again. The director followed up with her own welcome speech. It was getting late.

That night, no one could go to sleep right away, even though they all knew that bedtime in Artek really meant bedtime. The days were long, and silence usually descended quickly. Yet it was hard to be quiet with the new visitor in the dorm, and so everyone whispered, first in hopes that the whispers might reach the American girl, and then, realizing that she was fast asleep, just to each other, wondering what tomorrow might bring.

15

"THE WARRIORS OF THE INVISIBLE FRONT"

JULY 1983, CAMP ARTEK, USSR

It was Vladimir Mashatin's twenty-third trip to Camp Artek as the photographer for the *Pionerskaya Pravda* (Pioneer's truth), the country's main children's paper. In July 1983, his assignment was to photograph Samantha Smith, an American girl who had written a letter to Yuri Andropov.

"There is only you and your subject," Vladimir's photography teacher had told him many years before. "Whatever it is that you are shooting, think only of that." Vladimir clung to this mantra as he braved the winds of the Arctic, the sands of the Central Asian desert, and bureaucracies in towns big and small all over the Soviet Union.

When considering the best angle for the Samantha Smith assignment, Vladimir reckoned that Camp Artek would be the highlight of the little American's trip. He figured that the war monuments and museums of Moscow might not be as interesting to the eleven-year-old as children her own age might be. Artek had the Black Sea, the mountains, and all the extravagant shows usually held during the last days of the camp's sessions. He also knew that the Soviet government would limit its own reporters to allow for maximum international coverage and that in Moscow, where Samantha had an impressive entourage, he might not be able to get in on all the events. In Artek, however, as the photographer for the main children's newspaper, he was in his home territory. He was also very familiar with the camp's layout, having worked at Artek on many occasions. He knew that his pictures would stand out if he prepared well. Forgoing the documenting of the Smiths' arrival in Moscow on July 7, Vladimir flew to Artek—arriving in camp two days before the Smiths.

While Samantha and her parents toured Red Square and Lenin's Mausoleum, Vladimir toured Artek as the camp was preparing for the arrival of important guests. He made every effort to meet the staff working the session. In the morning, he introduced himself to the counselor of the Blue House and asked for a tour—even though he'd seen Artek's housing multiple times. At the Blue House, where Samantha would be staying, Vladimir also met a pair of "the warriors of the invisible front," as he dubbed the KGB agents from nearby Simferopol, who, like him, had arrived early to do some reconnaissance of their own.

He had long since learned the importance of Soviet intelligence agencies in the work of a reporter in the Soviet Union—and the need to be seen as nonthreatening to their superior task of "keeping order." His goal for the first two days of his stay in Artek was to ensure that his tall, slender frame and broad, friendly face became a familiar sight on the camp's grounds. He wanted the KGB to see him and note mentally, "This is the *Pionerskaya Pravda* reporter; he is here while Samantha is here. He is predictable; he presents no threat."

"As you see, we've been cleaning and cleaning," the counselor shared as the foursome walked down the hallways. They looked inside sunlit rooms where the beds were immaculately made; each pillow, as the camp tradition dictated, was placed on its side, with one corner tucked in, at the head of each camper's bed. The campers and counselors had been scrubbing the floors, washing windows, and making sure that everything and everyone looked presentable.

In the afternoon, Vladimir read through the camp schedule, mapping out the good locations where Samantha's interactions with the Soviet children could be captured most naturally. In the evening, he sat down for a chat and a cup of tea with his new KGB friends, who turned out to be quite sociable.

On the evening of July 9, when the Smiths arrived in Artek and Samantha decided she wanted to spend her first night with the campers, there was a mad rush to the Blue House. The reporters, campers, counselors, the KGB officers, Samantha, and her parents all ran there at high speed. This situation made getting a good shot challenging. To make matters worse, that night Vladimir learned that Arthur Smith had asked that Samantha be allowed to have fun with her peers and not be followed by the men with long lenses. "She is here as a representative of no one but herself," he said.

Of course, it made sense, but Vladimir had work to do and a story to tell. He was told that from then on, all permission to access the beach, camp cafeteria, and exercise field had to be secured in advance through official channels in Moscow. Thankfully, the task of enforcing the new rules was given to Vladimir's friends from the Simferopol KGB. As a reporter for the main children's newspaper (and by then a nonthreatening guy), he was given some leniency.

Yet, just to be on the safe side, the next morning Vladimir woke up early. By 6:00 a.m. he was at a spot he had scouted out the day before—under a cypress tree just off the exercise field where the campers' morning workout was going to start two hours later. He figured he would need the entire two hours, and he was right. Once he finished setting up his equipment, he noted two strangers in crisp white shirts on one of the nearby trails. The pair stood looking around and combing their hair every five minutes or so. Their manner was very casual, as if it were actually possible to enter the highly regimented and, due to the special guest's arrival, particularly secure grounds of Camp Artek. In a few minutes, a border patrol boat pulled up to the shore, and a few more men, also in white shirts but without the combs, walked up the trail toward him.

"You must leave the 'safe zone' immediately," they warned him.

"I'm the reporter for *Pionerskaya Pravda*," he answered, handing them his papers. He waited patiently as the men discussed "the situation" over their walkie-talkies. They used up his last hour verifying the authenticity of his journalist credentials, but in the end they left him alone under the cypress tree—just in time, too, for a few minutes later a loud horde of campers charged the exercise field.

The campers, all clad in swimsuits, lined up in several rows, saving the prized front-row spots for Samantha and her new Soviet friend, a girl named Natasha. Samantha, in a one-piece purple-polka-dot swimsuit, took her spot but seemed unsure of what was expected of her. Natasha, sensing that Samantha's "prized" spot effectively prevented her from being able to follow the person in front of her, tried to fix the problem by waving her arms up and down to show Samantha that she would have to jump. She pointed at the large speakers on the exercise field that would soon play the music. Samantha rubbed her nose, pushed her hair behind her ears, and nodded.

When the music started, Samantha made every effort to keep up and soon was jumping up and down with the music. As the morning exercise routine continued, Natasha carefully watched her new friend from under her arm, ready to help whenever Samantha appeared confused. Vladimir captured that look of care in the young Soviet girl's face for posterity.

Then, as the Artek schedule dictated, it was time for a brief morning swim before breakfast. Samantha ran into the water with the other kids. To Vladimir's surprise, the girl was completely unshaken by the fact that she had only met these children the night before—she splashed and laughed as the kids recited the Russian swimming rhyme about a granny who was planting peas. "Bab-ka see-ya-la go-rokh." Everyone jumped up and down to the words of the rhyme. "Ee ska-za-la grom-ko Oh!" When the granny loudly sighed "Oh!" in the last syllable of the rhyme, the campers and Samantha disappeared under the water. Vladimir was in awe of the girl's easygoing nature.

A few minutes later, with Samantha back on shore, Vladimir noticed a group of kids gathering around her. He rushed, sensing the possibility of a good shot. Sure enough, the boys had found a baby crab and were holding it up for Samantha to see. Vladimir started snapping. Then, suddenly, the little crab jumped out of one boy's wet hand. Surprised, Samantha also jumped, just as the shutter came down.

In the afternoon of that first day, another Artek activity was planned for Samantha: the bottle post. Also known as the "peace post," the bottle post was an old Artek tradition held once a year during the international session. The campers wrote down their wishes about friendship, peace, and getting along with others. Each camper then stuffed his or her wish into a bottle, sealed the bottle with wax, and brought it along on the boat that took them to the neutral waters off the Artek coast. With the shore out of sight, the campers would then toss the bottles into the sea.

As Samantha and her troop were writing their letters and stuffing them into bottles, Vladimir took his position at the boat terminal, where he knew they would be heading next.

Soon the traditional Artek chant went up in the air. "Artekovets sevodnia, Artekovets vseg-da!" ("Artek camper today, Artek camper forever!") shouted the campers as they lined up in two rows, welcoming Samantha and her troop. Samantha was wearing the white shirt and turquoise skirt of the Artek camp uniform by then but no red pioneer tie. In the camp uniform, she looked just like the other girls around.

Once on the boat, Vladimir grabbed a seat on the same side as Samantha and her parents. He was too far away to hear the conversations, but his lens let him get closer. He zoomed in past the multitude of campers' hats and snapped one of Natasha and Samantha—Natasha smiling, her finger pressed to her lips, as if saying, "Don't tell anyone!" He snapped pictures of campers taking pictures of Samantha and Samantha laughing in earnest or making a face in a surprised response to someone's comment. When it was time to toss the bottles into the sea, everyone cheered when the American girl's sacred wish joined theirs in the Black Sea.

Taking rolls and rolls of black-and-white film, Vladimir documented the campers trying to teach Samantha the words to their camp song, "Morskaya Dusha" (Sea Soul), about their Sea Camp and the Black Sea. Their arms around each other's shoulders, the campers rocked back and forth as they sang, "Sea Soul, Sea Soul, you are forever young."

Sam on the swing in Amity yard, 1977. (Courtesy of Jane Smith)

Sam, age four, at an animal farm in Houlton. (Courtesy of Jane Smith)

Jane and Arthur
with baby Sam,
Amity, summer
1972. (Courtesy
of Jane Smith)

Sam and Nonnie
(Arthur's mother,
Theresa) in the
fort they built
under the kitchen
table in Amity,
1974. (Courtesy
of Jane Smith)

Jane and Sam in Amity, winter 1975. (Courtesy of Jane Smith)

Amity Porch
(Bread bags in boots)

Little Sam on their porch in Amity. (Courtesy of Jane Smith)

Jane, Arthur, and Sam with their dog Kim, Manchester, Christmas 1982.
(Courtesy of Jane Smith)

Arthur and Sam being caught unaware in an old-fashioned photo booth for four
takes when they thought it would be only one! 1977. (Courtesy of Jane Smith)

Smith family and friends on the day of their departure to the Soviet Union. Manchester, July 7, 1983. (Collections of the Maine State Museum)

Sam, Jane, and Arthur at the Red Square. (DIOMEDIA / TASS Archive)

Sam in her Russian princess outfit. Natalia Batova on the left; Gennady Fedosov on the right. (Collections of the Maine State Museum)

Sam and Jane with Valentina Tereshkova, the first woman in space. (Collections of the Maine State Museum)

Smiths' arrival in Simferopol airport. (Courtesy of Vladimir Mashatin)

Samantha's arrival at Artek; Natasha on the far left, and Olga on the far right. (Courtesy of Vladimir Mashatin)

Samantha and Natasha on the beach in Artek. (Courtesy of Vladimir Mashatin)

Samantha and Natasha on the boat in Artek. (Courtesy of Vladimir Mashatin)

Samantha on the boat trip in Artek. (Courtesy of Vladimir Mashatin)

Samantha participating in the bottle post tradition in Artek. (Courtesy of Vladimir Mashatin)

Samantha with Olga in Artek, July 1983. (Courtesy of Olga Volkova)

Sam at her thirteenth birthday party, June 1985. (Courtesy of Jane Smith)

Troop #5, Camp Gaidarovets, summer 1983. I'm standing in the second row, sixth girl from the right. (Courtesy of Lena Nelson)

My mom, myself, and Baba Valia, New Year's 1977. (Courtesy of Lena Nelson)

My son Kenny at the Maine State Library and Museum in May 2006 with the Russian dolls, gifts to Samantha from the Soviet children. Baba Valia and I admired the one on the right when we saw a picture of Samantha with it in *Pionerskaya Pravda* in 1983. (Courtesy of Ken Nelson)

With Jane and my daughter Nikki, May 2006. (Courtesy of Ken Nelson)

16

"I LOVE YOU, ARTEK!"

JULY 1983, CAMP ARTEK, USSR

"I've sold you out, Sakhatova," said Valentin Saveliev, the Sea Camp director, to Olga Sakhatova, one of his Artek counselors. "You'll be working with Samantha."

"Why me?" Olga wondered out loud. "What have I done to deserve such punishment? It's such a huge responsibility!"

"You are the only camp counselor who can speak English, and you work at the Sea Camp, so that is why," the director replied.

The summer of 1983 was Olga's first at Camp Artek. A young English teacher from the Soviet republic of Turkmenia, Olga applied for the camp counselor position in Artek at a friend's suggestion. Her first year of teaching wasn't going so well: her students weren't interested in learning English, and she felt that maybe she was just too short or too skinny and, at times, way too lively for her students to take her very seriously. Of course, she also realized that she, too, would much rather play with the kids at breaks than drill the English tenses into them.

Going to Camp Artek had been her childhood dream, but despite her excellent grades and extensive extracurricular activities, she had never been selected. The daughter of a Soviet policeman and an accountant—not collective farmers or highly placed government officials, whose children were the usual candidates for a trip to Artek—she didn't fit the profile of a typical Artek camper.

It turned out that her chances of working there were much better. Having grown up in a multicultural family—her mother a Ukrainian, her father a Turkmen—Olga spoke Ukrainian, Turkmen, and Russian. She also knew English, which she had studied at university. With her coal-black hair and deep brown eyes, Olga was told, she represented the diversity of the Soviet republics. Her application stood out.

"It's a one-year contract but most likely two," a committee member told her at the interview, "so I hope nothing is holding you here." She hinted that a boyfriend might be a distraction.

"No, nothing's holding me here," Olga answered.

"Just don't end up in that horrid American land!" said Olga's grandma, spotting her granddaughter's growing excitement as she packed for Artek. She was traveling over thirty-five hundred kilometers away to a place where she might meet foreigners, who were nothing but trouble as far as her grandmother was concerned.

"Grandma, I'm going to Artek, not America!" Olga replied, but her grandma wasn't convinced.

Camp Artek was situated in the Crimean resort town of Gurzuf. Established in 1925, at the recommendation of the Russian Red Cross Society's chair as a sanitorium for children suffering from tuberculosis, it started as a tent camp but with time grew—in both size and popularity. By the 1980s, Artek was the most famous summer camp in the Soviet Union. It stretched over some 740 acres of the Black Sea coastline and had 150 buildings, including three medical clinics, its own school, a space museum, and even a film studio named Artekfilm. It also had three swimming pools, a seven-thousand-seat sports stadium, and various play-grounds available for year-round use.

Olga had heard of Samantha Smith's letter to Andropov and his invitation to Artek, but neither she nor the other counselors was ecstatic about the girl's imminent arrival. Since Samantha wasn't just any interna-tional camper but "the personal guest of the Soviet leader," a lot of work was being done to prepare. Renovations were going full-speed ahead. A giant palm tree was brought inside the cafeteria, and extra cleaning crews were dispatched to wash the floors and windows in the dorm hallways. Olga and the other counselors had been supervising the extracurricular activities, which included sweeping the roads leading to the dorms. Olga had already had a busy year and wasn't looking forward to this extra assignment, which had the potential to end badly.

As part of her initial Artek counselor training, Olga had spent four months living in the campers' dorms, following the camp's daily schedule, and doing arts and crafts just as her future charges would. She also studied child development, conflict resolution, and Artek history.

Having grown up in Turkmenia, a desert republic of the Soviet Union, where there was no air conditioning in the 1980s with summer temperatures above 45°C (113°F), Olga was always cold in Artek that first year—even in the summer. But she loved the beach and was particularly intrigued by the jellyfish that were abundant in the Black Sea. She'd never seen them before. Thinking that she should share the wonder of her discovery with her friends and family in Turkmenia, she decided to dry out a couple and send their skins in her letters back home. One afternoon, she caught a few of them and hid them in the rocks.

When she returned to check on them the next day, she discovered that they were gone.

"Someone stole my jellyfish!" she told a fellow counselor.

"What do you mean 'someone stole your jellyfish'?"

"Well, I put some among the rocks to dry out, and now they are gone!"

"You are kidding me, right? You do know that jellyfish are mostly water? They evaporated, silly!"

There were other things to learn—like more languages. Due to her already impressive linguistic abilities, after her training Olga was assigned as a counselor to the Sea Camp, which usually welcomed international sessions. For thirty days in the middle of summer, the Soviet campers lived side by side with children from other countries. Most international campers were from the Socialist Bloc countries, but the countries of Africa, as well as the capitalist nations of Belgium, Japan, Portugal, and the Federal Republic of Germany, among others, also sent children to Artek. A lot of the time those were the kids of peace activists or the grandkids of World War II veterans who believed in better understanding among peoples, which was the main goal of the international sessions.

Although exciting, international sessions came with extra responsibilities for the counselors. First, Olga had to make sure that the Soviet campers were on their best behavior—so as not to embarrass their motherland in front of the foreigners. That meant ensuring that the children were minding their manners, keeping their uniforms clean, and brushing their hair regularly. Then everyone needed to get along and follow camp rules—which was not so easy when the campers spoke different languages. The task was made even more challenging when the translators, who accompanied each foreign delegation, realized that Artek was in the middle of a resort town. They evaporated as quickly as the jellyfish in the Crimean sun, leaving Olga to figure out the multitudes of languages on her own.

That took time and ingenuity. One day, as she was trying to explain the words "Black Sea" to a camper from Mozambique, she kept pointing toward the water and repeating, "Chernoye Mor-re, Chernoye Mor-re." The camper followed her hand and, not seeing anything of significance in the distance, kept giving her a blank look. Then Olga lined up black and white checkers on the table. "Cherny," she pointed to the black one. "Bely," she pointed to the white one. "Cherny, bely, cherny, bely . . . Understand?"

"Si, señora," answered the boy.

"Chernoye Mor-re"—she pointed at the Black Sea again.

"Oh!" the boy said excitedly. "Mar Negro!"

She now knew how to say Black Sea in Portuguese.

She also learned that the directors of each delegation, who checked on the children weekly, had almost magic powers over their campers.

"Eating bien?" the Belgian group's director would ask during his weekly visits.

"Bien!" Olga would reply, having picked up the necessary vocabulary by then.

"Discipline? Bien?"

"Bien!"

If discipline wasn't so "bien"—something that occurred from time to time when children got too rowdy—she only needed to point out the camper in question. The director would give that child "the look" that seemed to fix almost any discipline issue. Olga didn't know how to ask what exactly the look implied, but she started calling it "the loud look." The kid got the message, and that was all that mattered when one had over thirty campers to monitor.

Soon Olga could say "Black Sea" and "Get a move on!" in Portuguese, French, German, and Japanese. Everything was going relatively well during that first international session—that is, until she was summoned to the office of the Sea Camp director and told that she'd be babysitting the personal guest of the Soviet leader.

As the day of the special guest's arrival approached, the counselors changed Samantha's name (a strange one by Russian standards) to Salamandra, which meant "salamander" in Russian—a slimy creature none of them were particularly fond of—for all the trouble her arrival was causing them. Now that Olga was tasked with babysitting Salamandra, she would have to leave the campers that she'd grown attached to and move to the Blue House, the newest dorm on the Sea Camp grounds, where the American guest would be staying. That was a particularly upsetting development.

"How is it possible," Olga thought to herself on the way back from the director's office, "that the general secretary invites someone to Artek, and I'm the one responsible for her? What if she falls and hurts herself?" Artek counselors were personally and legally responsible for their campers.

The camp administration had other things to worry about. The foreign press was expected to descend on Artek grounds, poised to ask questions of whomever they pleased. The "enemy journalists" (as the Western press was known in the Soviet newspapers) would go to great lengths to depict the Soviets in a bad light, so everyone had to remain vigilant. Special "political information" sessions were organized for the camp staff—to make sure that those not toeing the prescribed party line were much more aware of what was expected of them during the important guest's visit. The counselors were given strict instructions to stay out of the reporters' way and not to ramble about with the "enemy journalists"—to avoid any unnecessary problems.

Another responsibility that fell to Olga was tailoring the camp uniform on Natasha Kashirina, the girl who was going to welcome Samantha to Artek. Modifying the camp uniform, which was the camp's property, was against the rules. In fact, it was the counselor's job to account for every piece of it, and every lost cap, shirt, skirt, or pair of turquoise shorts would be deducted from the counselor's paycheck. Some counselors had very little coming their way at the end of summer, as the campers regularly lost their caps or left shirts and shorts on the rocks when they hunted for crabs on the beach. Olga diligently counted all the pieces of her campers' wardrobes almost on an hourly basis.

But Natasha had to look the part—the Western press would be ready with their cameras. So Olga rolled the hem of the skirt and sewed it up, although the result didn't look very attractive. Artek's deputy director confirmed her concerns.

"What's with the sausage at the bottom of the skirt?" she inquired. "Fix it!"

"But how? I can't cut the camp uniform," Olga protested.

"Go ahead and cut this one," the camp director insisted. Olga complied, cutting off a few centimeters and hemming the skirt neatly this time around.

On the day of the American guests' arrival, everyone was particularly on edge. The camp director must have asked Olga about a hundred times that day, "Be honest, Sakhatova, can you really speak English?" and she began to seriously doubt her English skills. "What if we don't understand each other? Then what?"

When the minivans carrying Samantha and her parents finally arrived in Artek, Olga was pleasantly surprised. The girl seemed lovely and even appeared a bit shy for someone who corresponded with the Soviet leader.

Olga came up to her and stretched out her hand.

"Hi, I'm Olga, your camp counselor."

"Hi," Samantha answered and shook Olga's hand.

Welcome ceremonies, replete with a Russian folk dance and bread and salt, were a resounding success. During the mad rush to the dorm, Olga tried to catch up with Samantha.

"Do you want to take a shower?" she asked Samantha.

"No, I'm OK," Samantha replied, and Olga breathed a sigh of relief. Samantha seemed to understand Olga's English, and Olga understood hers.

"This is the Blue House," the deputy director said, pausing at the entrance of Olga's new dorm and looking at Samantha.

"Do you want to stay with the children or with your parents tonight?" she asked.

"With the children," Samantha answered bravely.

Olga was impressed. Although only eleven and obviously tired after her long flight from Moscow, the girl seemed very open-minded about the strange things that were happening around her. Olga took it as a good sign: Samantha might not be as difficult a child as she had anticipated.

In the dorm that first night, Olga worried that getting sleep would be hard for her new charge. Earlier in the day, she had given explicit instructions to her campers: "Please, don't ask questions for the sake of asking. Don't bother her with picture taking and autographs. There are a lot of you here, and she is only one person. She is coming to have fun." Yet still she was worried that the girls in Samantha's room wouldn't be able to stop talking. Samantha handled that first night beautifully: when tired, she simply fell asleep.

Just before breakfast the next day, when Olga went to check whether everyone was ready for the trip to the cafeteria, she discovered that the Blue House girls had already dressed Samantha in the camp uniform and were now fixing her hair.

"She likes bows," they reported in unison, only momentarily looking up from their task of turning the long, white chiffon ribbons into *bantiki* (the traditional Russian bows) on Samantha's head. Samantha smiled the brightest, most satisfied and satisfying smile Olga had ever seen. As the campers shouted out commands to each other on how to beautify her further, Olga caught herself thinking that the girl didn't need any beautifying—with that smile on her face, the little American looked perfect.

At breakfast at the Sea Camp cafeteria, Olga realized that the campers had taken her earlier instructions to heart. Not only did they not want to get in trouble, but they also seemed genuinely invested in the idea that the American girl should have a good time in Artek, just like they did. The kids also seemed to enjoy being in Samantha's company. She was very animated as she tried to make herself understood: she waved her arms, drew circles in the air, and made faces. But she also listened attentively as the kids tried to explain something to her, only sometimes turning to ask, "Olga, what are they saying?"

Samantha was pretty, too, Olga thought, with a constant smile on her face, the type of smile the Soviets referred to as "Gagarin's smile," for Soviet cosmonaut Yuri Gagarin's notable smile—big, bright, and sincere, with eyes sparkling. She mentioned her observation to another camp counselor. He agreed but added, "But then again, they wouldn't send just any ugly crocodile over here, would they?" implying that maybe Samantha was handpicked for this moment. She did seem just too perfect a child for her presence to be an accident.

Yet Olga didn't worry too much about it. She, too, was discovering that Samantha was a lot of fun to be around. She was curious and uninhibited and keen on asking questions. Olga smiled when she wondered out loud about the high level of salt in the Black Sea.

"What's wrong with the water?" Samantha asked when she got out on shore.

"What do you mean?" Olga was confused.

"Why does it taste like that?"

"Salty? Do you mean salty? Don't you have salty water in the US?"

"Hmm, in the pond in Maine, where I swim, the water doesn't taste like that."

"Just don't drink the water, and it would be just like in Maine," Olga suggested. Samantha nodded in agreement.

It wasn't the questions themselves that surprised Olga—after all, not every eleven-year-old in the Soviet Union knew about the seawater being salty (she herself had just learned about jellyfish)—but the fact that Samantha was so comfortable with posing them whenever they occurred to her, without fear of coming across as silly or unintelligent. Olga's generation and that of her campers had been raised with an idea of "No questions!" That was true at school, where the teacher was an authority on any subject, and at the doctor's office, where doctors knew best. Watching Samantha ask questions about things big and small was refreshing.

Samantha had questions about other things—the color of the hotdogs in the Sea Camp's cafeteria, for example. At lunch, Samantha's new pal Natasha came running to the counselors' table. "Olga, I have no idea what she is saying. Come help!"

Olga found Samantha staring at the hotdogs on her plate.

"What are these?" she asked. If she had been asking about a local Russian dish, the question would have made sense to Olga, but hotdogs were supposed to be a popular American item, so Olga wasn't sure what exactly the problem was.

"Hotdogs," she answered.

"Hotdogs? But why are they yellow?" Samantha asked.

The hotdogs did look slightly anemic, but this was a time known as "deficit" in the Soviet Union, and once commonly available items had all but disappeared from the store shelves. In the United States, Olga reasoned, the hotdogs might have been made entirely from meat; in the Soviet Union, anything that even resembled a sausage or a hotdog was a welcome sight.

"Well, this is the type of hotdogs they have here," Olga said, hoping that the answer would satisfy her guest.

"Is it OK if I don't eat them?" Samantha asked.

"Of course, you don't have to eat them."

The assistant director of the cafeteria must have been watching Samantha's every move, because a few moments later she rushed over to the table with a large platter laden with crepes, jams, and cut fruit—in hopes of avoiding an international scandal. Samantha's eyes grew big at the sight of the giant platter. Did she have to eat everything on it?

"No, just as much as you want," Olga said with a smile.

"She doesn't like hotdogs?" asked the campers.

"I guess not," Olga answered.

The campers gave Samantha a strange look, but when she shared the items on the platter with them, everyone was happy. International scandal averted.

On that first full day in Artek, the camp administration tried to fit in as many events as possible: Olga accompanied Samantha on a bus tour of the camp, a walk through the camp museum, and then a tie ceremony at which Samantha received a blue guest tie—instead of the red pioneer tie—to wear with her camp uniform. Then there was the boat trip for the Artek bottle post.

The reporters kept their distance, and the camp counselors clearly took the director's earlier admonition in stride: none were seen near the reporters, even though the reporters did try to snap pictures from behind trees or buildings. One especially annoying "enemy journalist" was way too snoopy for Olga's taste—she kept spotting him here and there, trying to ask kids questions. Unfortunately for him, few of the children spoke fluent-enough English for a coherent interview.

In the evening, there was a meet-and-greet with the campers from different camps who had questions for Samantha about life in the United States, but the reporters, who attended the event, quickly took over and turned it into a press conference. Fortunately, the questions they asked seemed interesting to the campers.

"How do you like Artek?" asked one reporter. Samantha had been there only one day, but she was quick to respond that it was nothing like she'd expected.

"I thought it would be something like a nature camp, with tents and stuff, but it's completely different."

"So over there kids live in tents while in camp?" the campers whispered to Olga. "Like the ones we use when we go hiking?"

"I guess so," Olga seemed confused as well. All the summer camps she'd ever been to in the Soviet Union had cabins or buildings for campers to live in. Tents were for weekend camping trips with family or friends.

"What would you say if you could write a letter to your best friend right now?" asked another reporter.

"I'd say that I wish she could be here and that I'm having a lot of fun in Artek. I'd also tell her about things I'd seen in Moscow," Samantha replied.

"Who do you want to be when you grow up?" asked one of the reporters.

"A vet," Samantha answered.

"Why?" the kids whispered to Olga.

"I don't know," Olga replied.

"Do you play any sports?" asked another reporter.

Samantha said she liked softball. The campers looked at Olga puzzled again. They knew of football, basketball, and volleyball but had never heard of or seen the game of softball. It did help when the Smiths' translator compared it to the ancient Russian game of *lapta*, which was played with a wooden bat and a ball.

"I guess they use a bat to hit a ball with," Olga tried to explain.

"Huh?" The campers looked at her strangely: her explanation wasn't helpful.

Then a Soviet reporter asked Samantha what she'd do if she were a magician, and the question got lost in translation. Samantha looked at her dad, confused. He whispered something to her.

"Oh!" she exclaimed a second later. "Get rid of all the bombs, destroy bombs!" she said.

By nightfall of that first day in Artek, Samantha was exhausted. It was only her fourth day in the Soviet Union, and jet lag was hitting her hard. She asked to spend the night with her parents at the hotel nearby. She promised to return the next day.

The next morning, Samantha came with her mom, Jane, who was carrying a large bag of brightly wrapped candy to share with the campers. She asked Olga whether it would be OK to do so.

"It is, in fact, your duty to do so," Olga half joked. "The kids haven't seen this kind of candy and probably won't in the near future."

Jane gave the whole bag to Olga to share with the kids. With that gesture alone, Jane won Olga's heart. But she also had a beautiful smile and seemed gentle and funny, like her daughter. Brave too, Olga thought, to leave her child alone with complete strangers in a country so obviously different from theirs.

The government officials had planned a tour of the coast for them for the day. "Be good, Sam. Have fun!" Jane said before leaving.

Olga and Samantha spent most of the day outside. After lunch, unlike the other campers, Samantha and Natasha were allowed to skip the traditional quiet hour and instead roamed the Artek grounds and swam in the sea. For the first time that summer, Olga had only two campers to watch, and she spoke both of their languages.

The girls practiced rock skipping from the shore, which in Russian was called *blinchiki*, meaning "pancakes," a name Samantha found amusing. Soon, tired of rock skipping, the girls played with the jellyfish. They caught and arranged them by size on a towel.

"Aren't the jellyfish cute?" Samantha asked, holding one up as if it were a puppy.

"Jelly-fish?" Olga repeated—she'd never heard the English term for the sea creature. It made sense on closer consideration: "a fish that feels like jelly." Olga remembered her first encounter with jellyfish and smiled.

"They are mostly water. Toss them in so they don't dry out!" Olga admonished the girls.

When Samantha asked to practice the "Sea Soul" song she had learned the day before, the three of them sang it in Russian.

"What is your favorite children's song?" Olga asked.

"Children's song?" Samantha seemed confused. "I don't know any children's songs."

Olga was surprised. In the Soviet Union, there was an entire genre of songs that children learned in day care and school; there was even a famous Soviet composer, Vladimir Shayinskiy, who specialized in children's songs and melodies for Soviet cartoons. Every Soviet child had a favorite children's song.

"My all-time favorite song, though, is 'Edelweiss' from the movie *The Sound of Music*," Samantha said after a pause. "Have you seen it?" she asked.

Neither Olga nor Natasha had ever heard of the song or the movie, but when Samantha started singing, Olga was mesmerized by the melody and the lyrics. Hearing Samantha's little voice sing about the bright blossom, happy to meet her friend, seemed very fitting.

Soon enough, Olga realized that she wasn't alone in watching Samantha. On the beach, a young, suntanned lifeguard came up to them.

"Is this Samantha Smith?" he asked.

Olga nodded.

"Does she want a ride in my rowboat?"

"Yes!" Olga replied, excited. Then she turned to Samantha. "He wants to know if you want a ride in his boat."

"Yes!" Samantha got excited too.

A few minutes after they pushed off, a large motorboat pulled up next to them, and a very strict gentleman inquired why the American guest was without a life vest participating in an "unsanctioned activity." Olga had not been aware of the life vest rule. In fact, no one had ever required a life vest in any of the camp water activities before.

Picking up on the strained atmosphere of the exchange, Samantha asked why the man was so unreasonably serious. Olga supposed that he was most likely KGB, but instead she said, "He must be really hot and hence is grumpy for no reason."

The lifeguard turned his boat around and paddled to shore, where they got out. Olga never saw the good-looking lifeguard again. He was most likely fired soon afterward.

The next day, Artek celebrated Neptune Day, the highlight of any Soviet summer camp. On Neptune Day, the campers got a chance to dunk their counselors into the sea. The counselors and older campers dressed up as King Neptune's court: mermaids, sea witches, demons, and other undersea creatures that presumably came out of the water to hear campers' complaints, capture the evil counselors, and free the little children.

As the loud music played from the loudspeakers mounted on the shore, King Neptune walked down the pier, carrying a trident, and sat on his throne. Sea demons—with tails made of rope, their hair disheveled—leapt in wild dances around King Neptune and his daughters, the mermaids.

Olga had always wanted to be a mermaid for Neptune Day—to paint her legs in fish scales to resemble a mermaid's tail and wear a seaweed skirt. But here, too, she was given extra work to do: dressed in a long skirt and a shawl, her hair in a kerchief, she was the Gossip whose job was to collect the campers' complaints about their counselors.

She was walking up and down the beach recording campers' complaints when she spotted Samantha sitting in the crowd of campers completely bewildered by the antics on the makeshift stage.

"Do you have anything bad to say about your counselor? Speak now!" Olga jumped in front of Samantha. It took Samantha a moment to recognize Olga, but then she laughed out loud and said, "Nothing! Nothing!"

Then King Neptune got up from his throne, struck his trident three times, and ordered the sea demons to toss the offending counselors into the deep sea. The campers cheered, some running out to help the sea demons chase the counselors.

Olga's job, unfortunately, didn't exempt her from the king's punishment. She couldn't run very fast in that long skirt and heavy shawl. She, too, got picked up by her arms and legs, rocked back and forth, and tossed off the pier into the sea, shawl and all.

On Samantha's last day in Artek, their troop traveled to Yalta, where they visited the Livadia Palace Museum. In February 1945, the leaders of the United States, Great Britain, and the Soviet Union had met there for the Yalta Conference to discuss Germany's unconditional surrender and to plan for the postwar world. The museum's director let Samantha try out President Franklin Roosevelt's chair. It seemed symbolic to Olga that this little American girl, whom she had come to love by then, was sitting in the American president's chair during another tense time in history, the Cold War. She noticed how Samantha took care to place her feet firmly on the floor, managing to look all grown-up in this historic place.

That evening, Artek's closing ceremonies were orchestrated in Samantha's honor. They were especially lavish, as they were to be broadcast on all international news networks. An acrobat show and dance performances by children, all dressed as Misha, the mascot of the 1980 Olympic Games, were followed by the fireworks. By sunset, everyone was dancing. Samantha's father, Arthur, took part in a very active routine that required him to twirl in circles and clap his hands. Samantha's mom danced with the "enemy journalist," who then invited Olga for a spin. As the two of them clapped their hands and twirled, Olga realized that the "enemy journalist" was a perfectly nice and cheery gentleman. It had taken only three and a half days with the little American girl for Olga's own perceptions of the West to change drastically.

At the very end of the ceremonies, Samantha was invited to come up on stage. The campers pushed, trying to get close to her, and Olga watched as Natasha put her arm around her to keep her steady. They sang Artek's farewell song:

> Quietly the last ambers melt in the campfire.
> It's time for us to say Farewell.
> Friends, hand me a dazzling amber from this fire.
> The evening is drifting in the moonlight,
> The winds carry our song to the stars.

Then it was Samantha's turn to speak. She came up to the microphone: "My stay at Sea Camp in Artek has been wonderful. Very wonderful. I shall miss my new international friends. But we will remain friends across the sea. Let our countries be friends too. Someday I hope to return. I love you, Artek!"

17

"SO DO THE RUSSIANS WANT WAR?"

JULY 1983, MOSCOW, USSR

"Why are the Soviet people so taken by Sam?" Arthur and Jane, surprised by all the attention, asked Natalia Batova, the Soviet diplomat and interpreter who was accompanying them on their tour. Indeed, in July 1983, Samantha Smith was the main attraction wherever she went in the Soviet Union. In Moscow and now in Leningrad, crowds gathered at every event she attended. In towns all over the Soviet Union, one could see her on the evening news broadcasts and in the newspapers.

When, the previous spring, Yuri Andropov's Secretariat office had received the news from the Soviet embassy in the United States that the Smith family had accepted the Soviet leader's invitation to tour the Soviet Union, Natalia Batova, then secretary of the USSR-USA Society, was called to a meeting with the representatives of the Youth Organizations Committee and state television and radio. There, along with several other Soviet officials, she was tasked by the Ministry of Foreign Affairs with preparing the itinerary for the Smiths' visit. The assignment was unique: she was to host an eleven-year-old personal guest of the Soviet leader. Furthermore, the story had already received unprecedented news coverage.

Natalia had worked for the USSR-USA Society for over ten years by the time the Smith assignment landed on her desk. A 1970 graduate of the Moscow Institute of International Relations, Natalia spoke English fluently, had overseen visits of many delegations from the West, and had herself traveled to the United States several times as a participant in Soviet-American exchanges.

Natalia had followed the story of Samantha's letter in the news: her twelve-year-old daughter, Alyona, was only one year older than Samantha. She was impressed with the poignant question Samantha asked the Soviet leader: "Do you plan to start a war?" Short and to the point, thought Natalia, and very reflective of the climate of the day. Like many Soviet diplomats, Natalia hoped to find a way of changing what she deemed an erroneous impression of her compatriots and their way of life. She wanted to show Samantha and her family, along with all Americans, that the Soviets did indeed want peace and mutual understanding.

When Natalia first saw Samantha at the Sheremetyevo airport, she was surprised by how at ease the girl was with the cameras and questions coming her way. Over thirty reporters and their crews had gathered in a small waiting area. Concerned that the family might be tired after their long trip, Natalia warned the reporters, "We will need to keep it short."

When one of reporters asked Samantha what she might say to Yuri Andropov if she got to meet him, Samantha didn't look at her parents for advice, responding, "He promised me he wouldn't start a war. Americans say they won't start a war either. Then how come we keep making bombs for war if there is no one to start it?"

Natalia was impressed with this child's clarity of thought: even after such a long trip, she had the presence of mind to grasp the question and articulate her answer precisely. Natalia told Arthur and Jane as much: "That is inspiring and surprising at the same time."

With each day, Natalia was finding her assignment more and more fascinating. An experienced diplomat, she was learning from an eleven-year-old, a notion she herself found astonishing.

The itinerary they prepared wasn't for the faint of heart. While in Artek, Arthur and Jane were able to relax somewhat: they visited botanical gardens and a winery on the Crimean coast and spent time at the beach. Samantha, as the guest of honor at many camp events, didn't get much of a break. Reporters and cameramen followed her every move.

At yet another press conference in Artek, Natalia looked around the room and thought, "An eleven-year-old is holding a press conference. By herself."

"What do you think of Artek?" asked one reporter.

"I'd love it if American kids had a camp like that," she answered.

Natalia listened carefully—to translate but also to try to figure out how she would have answered the questions.

"What did you think of the Soviets?" asked another reporter.

"They are very much like us, the Americans," Samantha answered without skipping a beat. A radical concept in the Cold War era, Natalia thought. Samantha had spent only a few days in the company of the Soviet kids but had already come to an important conclusion.

In moments like this she was truly taken aback by the girl's lightning-quick reaction to the question and her ability to compose an answer that smoothed out any "sharp edges." Such freedom of thought and the ability to express it without looking to anyone for support or approval, Natalia thought, was impressive for anyone, let alone a child.

By their last day in Artek, exhaustion was catching up with Samantha: the cameras caught a glimpse of her in the crowd of children trying to stay awake as everyone watched yet another event, a swimming competition. The next morning, at a state-run experimental collective farm that the Smiths stopped at on their way to Simferopol airport, Samantha and her friend Natasha from Artek ate fruit right from the trees and had lunch with the farm director's family. It was there, in the farm's garden, that Samantha let slip in front of the cameras, "I can't wait till the trip is over. . . . I'm homesick," she said in a soft voice, almost apologetically.

By the time they arrived in Leningrad, the rigorous schedule of several events per day, each one lasting two to three hours, had resumed. And while the parents could pick and choose which of them would accompany Samantha to a particular event, Samantha had to go to each one. Or it would be cancelled.

"We had clearly overdone it with the schedule," Natalia would remark years later. Even an adult would have found it difficult. On their first day in Leningrad, they went to the Piskaryovskoye Cemetery, a solemn place where the victims of the nine-hundred-day German siege of Leningrad were buried. Samantha laid a wreath and learned the story of eleven-year-old Tania Savicheva, a girl who kept a diary during the siege recording the deaths, one after another, of her entire family. "The Savichevs are dead. All are dead. Tanya is the only one remaining." The visit was meant to remind the world of the Soviet sacrifice during World War II. The atmosphere was somber, but Samantha rose to the challenge—understanding how to behave and be thoughtful in a place of deep sadness and memory.

Next, they drove to the House of Friendship and Peace, a branch of the Soviet Cultural Society for the Relations with Foreign Countries, where they watched a film on the horrors of World War II, once again emphasizing the idea that the Soviets wanted peace. From there, in a rapid succession, there was a trip to the Smolny Institute, Vladimir Lenin's headquarters during the 1917 October Revolution, and then to the battleship *Aurora*, whose cannons had heralded the beginning of the revolution. As hundreds of Soviets crowded around the entrance to the ship to see Samantha, one of the *Aurora* sailors presented her with a bouquet of red carnations. At the end of the tour, the captain gave her a ceramic polar bear, a sailor's blue-and-white kerchief, and a ship's badge.

At every location, there were flowers or gifts. Samantha smiled, graciously accepted the gifts, and followed her hosts to hear yet another presentation in Russian with English translation—which made the event twice as long. At Leningrad Pioneer Palace, a gathering place for Soviet youngsters to pursue dance, photography, and handicrafts, she dutifully watched Russian folk dancing and was presented with an embroidered apron, a papier-mâché peacock, a white crocheted purse, and a set of stuffed animals that the kids had made for her.

Natalia noticed how capable Samantha was under pressure. Even though, just a few minutes earlier in the hotel room, she might have looked tired or unsure as to what they were going to see next, as soon as she faced the cameras, she assumed the look of a seasoned diplomat—to Natalia's great amazement. She smiled, shook hands, asked and answered questions. Over and over again, the little girl pulled herself together and put her best foot forward. "There are diplomats among us," thought Natalia to herself, "who could learn from her."

But most of all, Natalia was inspired by the power of Samantha's sincerity and kindness—she smiled at strangers on the street as they waved to her or took the time to listen to the kids whose language she didn't understand. She did indeed have the rare intuition of a true pro.

"She'd make a great diplomat someday," Natalia told Jane and Arthur.

As Natalia observed the Smiths, she saw why Samantha had such presence and confidence. Her parents were supportive of her quest. Seeing this trip as Samantha's personal mission, they followed along, only facilitating the opportunity. They were available but not interfering. And when Natalia watched the way Arthur and Jane interacted with each other, she felt sometimes like she was watching a beautiful film.

One day in Leningrad, Samantha asked Natalia whether she could bring her roller skates with her to one of the events, hoping to go roller-skating with the Soviet kids. Few kids owned roller skates in the Soviet Union, Natalia told her. "But maybe we could sneak out of the hotel very early tomorrow morning, before anyone else is up, and I can take you skating by the Neva River?" she offered. Samantha loved the idea.

The next morning, bright and early, before the press was up and when hardly anyone was out on the streets of Leningrad, Natalia and Jane took Samantha roller-skating on the Neva River embankment.

In Leningrad, Samantha met up with Natasha Kashirina, who had just arrived home from Artek, and the two girls went to the Kirov Ballet, where they watched *The Fountain of Bakhchisarai*. At intermission, Samantha was taken backstage to meet the famed Soviet ballerina Alla Sizova, who presented her with signed pointe shoes.

In Leningrad, Natalia noticed how close Samantha had become to "Little Natasha," as Natasha Kashirina became known (Natalia now being referred to as "Big Natasha"). It was as if in "Little Natasha," Samantha saw a haven from the hustle and bustle of adults who wanted to discuss yet another stop on their itinerary. With Natasha, Samantha could be a kid, and she held on to that, spending a good part of their evening trying on pointe shoes and dancing.

The next day, there was a trip to Petrodvorets, Tsar Peter the Great's summer residence. An expansive complex of gilded palaces and gardens dating back to the 1700s, Petrodvorets boasted the golden Grand

Cascade fountain and multitudes of smaller ones, including some prank fountains, which the tsar installed for the amusement of his courtiers. As Natalia looked on, the girls dashed down the garden pathway, hopping around the rocks and trying to avoid accidentally setting off a fountain and getting soaked. When they finally did get soaked, they only laughed harder and made several more dashes, giggling all the way. In the evening, there was yet another outing: to the Hermitage Museum, one of the world's largest art museums. When it was time for Samantha to return to their hotel and for Natasha to head home, Samantha broke down in tears—she didn't want to say good-bye.

"We have a train to catch," reminded Arthur. But Sam just wanted to spend a little more time with Natasha.

The next morning, after an eight-hour overnight train trip, the Smiths arrived at the Moscow train station, where they were met by the customary limousine and a police escort.

Natalia decided to cancel some of the planned activities for that day, reserving only the trip to the circus, which Samantha was looking forward to. Natalia could see Samantha needed a break. Samantha's favorite act that night was an acrobat who did a backward flip on stilts.

On Monday, July 18, Natalia accompanied the Smiths to the Soviet Women's Committee, where Samantha, Jane, and Arthur met with Valentina Tereshkova, the first woman cosmonaut, who twenty years earlier had made a seventy-hour flight orbiting Earth. Tereshkova showed them her collection of one hundred dolls from all over the world and then served tea with cookies, after which the family posed for pictures. They then continued to the Olympic stadium, where Samantha and Arthur were persuaded to bike around the Olympic cycling track at the Krylatsky Sports Complex's velodrome. The track was steep, but Samantha was game. After a lengthy bike adjustment, she took off all by herself with two Soviet athletes following her closely.

From there, they followed their guides to the gymnastics hall, where they watched the Soviet gymnasts perform. There Samantha got to participate—she did summersaults on the floor and a short routine on the balance beam.

The next day, July 19, was their final outing to Red Square, followed by a trip to the Novodevichy Monastery, where Tsar Peter the Great imprisoned his half sister Sophia, and then on to Moscow State University and the Bolshoi Theater. There was also a stop at the Natalia Durov animal theater, which had to be cut short—to Samantha's great dismay; she had been hoping to vote for her favorite animal performer. Next on the schedule was a visit to the Spasso House, the official residence of the American ambassador to the Soviet Union, Arthur Hartman. Natalia learned that Samantha, while still disappointed about the abridged animal theater trip, brightened up considerably when she saw that hamburgers and fries were on the menu at the American embassy.

On the Smiths' last full day in Moscow, Wednesday, July 20, the media speculated that the meeting with Andropov was imminent. The reporters couldn't help but notice the Smiths' more formal attire: in the morning, Arthur emerged in a suit, Jane wore a long-sleeved dress, and Samantha put on a skirt and tied her hair up with a Russian bow.

Throughout the entire trip Samantha kept asking, "Do you think there will be a meeting at the Kremlin?"

Natalia also wanted to know, but no information was forthcoming. The meeting wasn't confirmed, but there hadn't been word that it wouldn't happen either. She was hopeful, as it definitely would be the highlight of a very successful trip—a real breakthrough, in her opinion.

Only one event had been planned for that last day—luncheon at the Moscow Pioneer Palace—just in case. On the way there, as Natalia sat next to Samantha in the backseat of the limousine, she noticed Samantha looking down at Natalia's shoes.

"What is your shoe size?" she asked Natalia.

"Thirty-seven, but in US it would be six and a half," Natalia answered.

"Hmm, that could be my size," Samantha pondered out loud, measuring her foot against Natalia's. "Can I try on your shoe?"

Natalia smiled, remembering how her daughter Alyona also loved to try on those wedges—heels not too high so as to wobble but high enough to feel all grown up.

"Sure." Natalia took off her shoe and helped Samantha put it on.

"Can I try the other one?"

Natalia took off the second one. As they pulled up to the Pioneer Palace, the crowd of reporters was at the ready.

"Can I wear them today?" whispered Samantha.

"Of course," Natalia answered and quickly put on Samantha's sandals. Then she opened the door and watched Samantha hop out and stride confidently toward the reporters in her heels.

At the Moscow Pioneer Palace, Samantha was presented with an exquisite Russian costume made especially for her. When she tried on the embroidered *sarafan* (the Russian national dress) and the pearl-decorated crown, or *kokoshnik*, Natalia and everyone around her gasped: Samantha looked like a beautiful Russian princess.

Later in the day, they received a call from Andropov's office. He would be sending his deputies with gifts for Samantha and family. This meant that there would be no meeting. The news reported that he had a meeting with the Hungarian leader Janos Kadar that day. Samantha pursed her lips; her face got long. She sighed.

A few hours later, a delegation of Andropov's deputies, headed by Leonid Zamyatin, chief of the Kremlin's International Information Department, arrived bearing gifts—a large box with a Russian samovar bearing Andropov's personal card; a lacquered Palekh box, its lid decorated with a delicate painting of a racing troika; a gold-trimmed tea set; and a one-hundred-page photo album of Samantha's stay in the Soviet Union. Samantha gave them a signed book of Mark Twain's speeches, which she and her parents had picked out for Andropov in the States—a gift they had managed to keep secret from the reporters.

The next morning, Natalia brought an extra pair of shoes to work. In the Smiths' hotel room, she handed Samantha her wedges, the ones that she wore to the Moscow Pioneer Palace. "Here, they're yours now!"

At the press conference an hour later, surrounded by microphones and lights, Samantha fielded more questions from reporters.

"Were you disappointed that you didn't get to meet with Yuri Andropov?" asked one.

"No," she said thoughtfully. "I mean, he sent his deputies over to our hotel. That's good enough."

"Was there any message from Mr. Andropov?" reporters persisted.

"He said that he was sorry that he couldn't meet with me, that he was just too busy. And he wishes me hope for no war and good health."

"Did he pass any message to the officials of the United States, perchance?"

"No," Sam answered.

"Do Americans have a wrong idea about the Soviet Union?"

"Some of them do. But the people who have been to the Soviet Union have a definite answer—them not wanting war at all, and them wanting peace. Just like I do."

"How does it feel to be a center of attention?"

"When you're just sitting here, it's not difficult, but when you are trying to go somewhere . . ." She recounted their time in Montreal. "We had policemen surrounding us, and the photographers just crushed right through them. I ended up biting one of the microphones."

"So, what do you think now—do the Russians want war?" asked another reporter.

"No," Samantha smiled widely and shook her head.

When asked by the Associated Press of the family's plans, Arthur concluded, "I just want to get home and get myself reoriented."

Samantha had a better idea: "If my best friend Lynn doesn't meet me at the airport, I'm going to go home and call her up and tell her to come see me."

That afternoon, Natalia led the Smiths to the gate of their Aeroflot flight for Montreal and helped the three check in a total of fourteen pieces of luggage—all gifts, except for the things they had brought with them.

18

"SAMANTHA PUT THE SOVIETS IN COLOR"

JULY 1983, ARKHANGELSK, USSR / JULY 2017, SIMI VALLEY, CALIFORNIA

By the time I returned home from Camp Gaidarovets, Samantha had left the Soviet Union. At camp, I'd seen a couple of nightly news broadcasts of Samantha, but I wanted to know more: I was curious to learn what she thought of the Soviet Union. Baba Valia handed me a stack of newspaper clippings she had saved for me. She pointed at the pictures of her in Camp Artek and read the interviews out loud.

"Samantha, who do you want to be when you grow up?"

"A hairdresser or a vet. I want to know what the animals are thinking about."

"What would you like to wish to all the kids in the world?"

"To live with the hope that there will be no war. Now I live with this hope."

"Samantha, what would you do if you were a magician?" Baba Valia read, imitating a reporter's voice.

"I'd destroy all the bombs. I now think that the Soviet people also don't want war," she tried to read in an upbeat kid's voice.

"See? It was good that she came to Artek," said Baba Valia, reminding me of the time I was jealous and not so sure about the Camp Artek invitation for Samantha.

Baba Valia was particularly excited about a picture of Samantha holding a doll in a Russian folk costume that was given to her as a gift in Artek. The caption under the picture read, "We were saddened to hear Samantha's response to our question about whether she liked dolls. She replied that she didn't really like to play with dolls. Yet she really loved the doll in the beautiful Russian national costume that was a gift from the young reporters of the *Pionerskaya Pravda*. She named her Natasha."

Baba Valia pointed at Samantha. "Look at her smile! She doesn't like dolls, but she liked the Russian one!" Baba Valia was as proud as if she had made the doll and the folk costume herself.

I still wasn't sure whether Samantha's question about whether the Soviet people wanted to start a war warranted a trip to Camp Artek, but I felt good that she believed the answer was no. I was glad that this American girl liked the Soviet people. Back then I did not know or ask whether this was what Yuri Andropov had hoped for: that Samantha and her parents would see that Soviets had a lot in common with Americans and that they would tell others. Jane's brother Hank said it well years later: "Samantha put the Soviets in color. Before her trip I saw only black-and-white propaganda—only that they all were living in the past, acting like there was no color. Not only in the way of their TVs but generally—like even their grass was grey. And when Sam went there, we saw that it was green."

Decades later, I don't really know whether Yuri Andropov intended for the Soviet citizens to see that Americans also could be friendly, but in the summer of 1983 the window of that possibility opened for me— never to be shut again: if there was one friendly American family, chances were there were more of them. And they, too, didn't want a war.

In 2013, for the thirtieth anniversary of Samantha's trip to the Soviet Union, I was working on an article about Samantha for the *Bangor Daily News* and reached out to former Soviet president Mikhail Gorbachev, who in the spring of 1983 was considered Andropov's protégé. When Andropov was ill, Gorbachev presided over several Politburo sessions, possibly including the one that discussed Samantha Smith's letter and Andropov's response. I wanted to know why Yuri Andropov and the Soviet government decided on this extraordinary step. I also asked about what he thought of Samantha's contribution to Soviet-American relations.

On Facebook, I found Mikhail Gorbachev's interpreter, Pavel Palazhchenko, and inquired whether I could get President Gorbachev's thoughts on Samantha's letter. I was pleasantly surprised to receive a response and a request for questions. A few weeks later, I received the answers and the permission to quote. In his response, Mikhail Gorbachev said:

> *Samantha Smith wrote her letter to Yuri Andropov at the time when the Cold War was at its peak. Years had passed since the last meeting of the Soviet and American leaders. Missiles that could reach their target in five minutes were being deployed in Europe. It was the sincerity of Samantha's letter that garnered everyone's attention. We understood at the time that people on both sides of the ocean were very concerned; they wanted to make sure that both Soviet and American leaders understood that concern. An American girl was able to express that concern in her letter. Of course, because of Andropov's illness there was no discussion of him meeting with Samantha, and it's unlikely that it would have been possible at such a time in history. What was important is that the voice of an ordinary, young person had been heard.*

But what did the American government think of Samantha's diplomatic efforts? Why did neither President Ronald Reagan nor any of his staff publicly acknowledge Samantha's correspondence with Yuri Andropov—even when it drew such unprecedented international attention?

By the summer of 2017, I'd corresponded with Jenny Mandel, the archivist at the Ronald Reagan Presidential Library in Simi Valley, California, for close to two years, and it looked like everything to be found on Samantha Smith at the library had already been scanned and sent my way. At that time, the White House Office of Records Management subject file titled "Peace" had one case file on Samantha. It contained mostly letters from state representatives forwarding their constituents' inquiries about Samantha to the White House as well as drafts of responses—some dated in the spring-summer of 1983; others, after Samantha's death in 1985.

One such letter sent to the White House on April 26, 1983, a day after Samantha received Andropov's response, was a Western Union Mailgram from Mr. and Mrs. Donald Jelks of Maitland, Florida. The Jelkses suggested that President Reagan take Samantha, as "the dove of peace," with him to Moscow for an impromptu meeting with Andropov. "You take her, her parents, a few friends, and Mrs. Reagan to Moscow without a great entourage of staff or planning. . . . [T]ake only one reporter from each network and major newspaper [and] a very limited number of government officials."

The president's assistant, Anne Higgins, reviewed the Mailgram and prepared a response. "The Administration firmly believes in the importance of communication between our two societies," Higgins wrote. "We believe that those Americans who travel to the USSR, as Samantha will, can benefit from first-hand exposure to the Soviet system. We sincerely hope that the Soviet citizens will someday enjoy the same freedom to travel and to become familiar with other societies." But, Higgins noted, "a failure to communicate is not at the heart of the difficulties between our two countries." "Viewed realistically," she continued, "the issues on which the US and the USSR disagree are complex ones that are not subject to resolution with a few bold diplomatic strokes."

Another letter in the case file was from Mr. Morton P. Matthew from Litchfield, Connecticut, who suggested that President Reagan invite a Soviet child for a reciprocal visit to the United States. "I can't think of anything more appropriate, more inspiring, or more likely to be a hairline crack in the iron-uranium wall between east and west," he wrote on July 11, 1983, when Samantha was in Artek. His letter made it to the desk of Alvin Paul Drischler, acting assistant secretary of legislative and intergovernmental affairs. In September 1983, Drischler responded:

As you may be aware, this proposal was recently considered by the Administration. It was decided, however, that such a gesture would not be proper at this time. The primary reason for this decision was

that highly visible and well-publicized visits of this type tend to give
a misleading impression about Soviet policies. They create an impres-
sion that genuine, large scale, and free exchange of ideas, people and
information with the Soviet Union are possible, when in fact as a
result of Soviet actions they are not.

The Soviet Union, Drischler continued, "has waged an increasingly successful campaign to isolate its people from outside influences, and to restrict the free flow of information, ideas and people across its borders," while continuing "to maintain that it respects the understandings embodied in the Helsinki Final Act, including pledges to facilitate human contact." "This Administration," Drischler concluded, "will continue to do what it can to encourage the Soviets to increase contacts between all its people and the outside world, while avoiding actions which would foster an erroneous impression of present Soviet policies."

Higgins and Drischler were right: By 1983, we Soviets were indeed isolated, so much so that when I first saw Samantha and her family on my black-and-white TV, I felt like I was watching aliens from another planet. But Samantha and everyday Americans had the same perception of us, the Soviets. People on either side of the Iron Curtain knew very little about each other's worlds and lived in great fear because of it. So when Mr. Drischler suggested the need to "encourage the Soviets to increase contacts between all its people and the outside world" but argued that "highly visible and well-publicized visits" like Samantha's only "foster[ed] an erroneous impression of present Soviet policies," I disagreed. Samantha's trip did just what he said couldn't be done: it proved that "free exchange of ideas, people and information" was possible when common people met. Does the preservation of peace rest solely in the hands of the governments?

As I expanded my search of the files at the Ronald Reagan Presidential Library, I was particularly interested in the collection of Jack F. Matlock, who in the summer of 1983 had become special assistant to the president and senior director of European and Soviet affairs at the National Security Council. Matlock, an avid scholar of the Soviet Union, would go on to serve as US ambassador to the Soviet Union and to witness the crumbling of the Soviet Empire. Matlock's files at the Ronald Reagan Presidential Library filled seventy-five boxes.

"There is no folder title for 'Samantha Smith' but possibly an exhaustive examination of the collection might locate a document," replied Jenny to yet another of my inquiries. "You are welcome to come and examine the collection, particularly if you believe that the Reagan White [House] did have a role in Samantha's visit to and relationship with the USSR."

In July 2017, I studied the twenty-one pages that described the documents in the boxes of the Matlock collection and highlighted the case files that looked promising. I knew it was wishful thinking, but I thought it was worth a try.

On arriving at the library's research wing, I went through a brief orientation, picked up my Ronald Reagan Presidential Library researcher card, and settled in at one of the long tables. When the cart with boxes I requested arrived, I started at the top of my long list.

I slowly thumbed through numerous briefing proposals and memos, excerpts from speeches by Leonid Brezhnev, Yuri Andropov, and Soviet foreign minister Andrei Gromyko, as well as summaries of the 1983 meetings between George Shultz and Anatoly Dobrynin that I'd read about in their memoirs.

There was a long document titled "Soviet Strategy to Derail US INF Deployment—an Intelligence Assessment" and a memo Jack Matlock addressed to William Clark on the impact of leaks on the government's ability to deal with the Soviets: "If we are to have hope of establishing useful dialogue with the Soviets, we are going to have to demonstrate that we can in fact keep our conversations out of the public eye or else the Soviets will systematically avoid conveying any views to us which deviate from their public position."

As I worked through the boxes and folders, I came across drafts of Reagan's June 1983 letter to Andropov congratulating him on becoming chairman of the Presidium of the USSR Supreme Soviet—with sentences crossed out for clarity, approved, and reapproved before the final version was sent to its intended recipient. In one folder I found a list of areas closed to Soviet citizens subject to travel regulations. It included the entire length of the Mississippi River and ten counties in Maine. In the 1980s,

Riverside County, California, where I now lived, would potentially have been off limits to me had I, then a holder of a Soviet passport, happened to visit in the "framework of US-USSR exchange." I would have had to notify the Department of State, providing my "itinerary, identification of means of transportation used, route numbers of all roads traveled by car listed in the order in which the roads [were] taken, and the location of each overnight stop." I knew that those regulations were reciprocal—American citizens couldn't come to Arkhangelsk in the 1980s. "We've come a long way," I thought. "Here I am, a former Soviet citizen, looking through confidential memos at the Ronald Reagan Presidential Library."

Hours had passed, and, while fascinating, none of the files I looked through mentioned Samantha. I was about to call it a day, somewhat disheartened, but decided I could work through one more box. Halfway through Box 26, in the last of the five beige folders titled "USSR General—1981–1983," I came across a National Security Council confidential memo of August 9, 1983.

"Proposal to Invite Soviet Youth to U.S.," read its subject line. "This must be the proposal to invite a Soviet child to the United States discussed in Drischler's response," I thought. Two pages in, the subject line of another document read, "Samantha Smith and Avi Goldstein."

As I turned the pages, I learned that at around the same time Sam and Natasha were playing in the Black Sea, Michael Gale of the White House Office of Public Liaison, Jewish Affairs, drafted a proposal that he hoped would help "combat some of the news coverage on Samantha Smith." The proposal's centerpiece was a letter from a nine-year-old Avi Goldstein in Tbilisi, USSR, written just two weeks after news of Andropov's reply to Sam's letter broke.

An open letter to the lucky American girl who received a letter from Mr. Andropov himself,

Dear friend,

My name is Avi Goldstein. I am about your age, was born in December 1973. I live in Tbilisi, USSR. My parents applied for exit visas to Israel two years before I was born and got refused their right

to emigrate. So I have experienced a lot: imprisonment of my uncle in 1978, searches of our apartment, etc. The goal of my letter is not to make you pity me, not at all. I just want you to forward my letter to Mr. Andropov because he never answered my letter sent directly to him. He is nice enough to invite you to pioneer camps at the Black Sea shore in the USSR, but he denies my right to travel to Israel. Double standard approach to children may suggest double standard approach to serious problems. I wouldn't like to think so. Let us imagine that Mr. Andropov hasn't received any of my letters, and if he did, he would order to let our family go—at least me and my mother or me and my grandmother. All of these combinations have been tried with no success. Once again, I ask you, my American friend, to make this letter known to Mr. Andropov. Having a precedent already, you are to expect an answer this time also. The answer could be exit visas for my family. If so, you won a victory—in the human right's fight. If not, you know more about human hypocrisy.
Hoping to hear from you soon,
Sincerely,
Avi Goldstein.
PS My parents helped me to compose this letter in English.

Michael Gale proposed the following:

What I would like to do is to arrange for a letter to come from Avi to President Reagan, which can be obtained around the first of August through some tourists bound for Tbilisi. This letter could be followed by a letter of invitation from the President to visit the United States, which would most likely be denied. This denial can then be used to dramatize the President's concern for human rights. If the Soviet Union permits Avi to come, or even if he is denied, we will [have] a great opportunity available to us.

Avi's letter addressed the real human rights issues that formed one of the main reasons for Reagan's distrust of the Soviets. Yet the attempt by highly placed government officials, who had diplomatic solutions at their fingertips, to use the Goldstein family's hardship seemed manipulative. After all, Samantha's trip was a positive development in Soviet-American relations, as stated by US Ambassador Arthur Hartman, who, on meeting the Smiths, said that Samantha's visit "reflects very favorably on America. Her exposure here is a plus for us." He added, "Everyone can agree with her brand of peace."

Were members of President Reagan's staff really that concerned about eleven-year-old Samantha receiving an unparalleled amount of news coverage that seemed, for a time, to overshadow the president's own efforts for cooperation with the Soviets? Did Samantha's correspondence with Andropov come at a time when Reagan hoped to have his own breakthrough with the Soviet leadership?

By then, I knew that the Smiths were concerned about the plight of the "refuseniks," as individuals denied Soviet exit visas were then known, and had handed their letters to the Soviet officials on their arrival in Moscow. That was all they could do at the time as the guests of the Soviet government.

Jack Matlock and John Lenczowski of the National Security Council also had concerns about the proposal regarding Avi's letter. While Matlock thought that, in principle, the idea was excellent, he worried about "any White House involvement in getting the letter here."

> *If the direct letter doesn't arrive, could we proceed on the basis of the open letter we have already? I assume we are convinced that the open letter itself is bona fide. What do we know about Avi and his family? Should we check out the facts as completely as we can before making a commitment? Also, we should let State know what is afoot and see if they have any advice.*

Two weeks later, on August 9, 1983, by which time Sam was back in Maine, Lenczowski wrote, "The proposal entails too many drawbacks. Not only are there problems with White House complicity in arranging for the boy's letter and using amateurs to obtain, but we have problems with mimicking the crude Soviet attempt to exploit a child for blatant propaganda purposes."

Thirty-some years later, there is no way of knowing whether the proposal made it to President Reagan's desk or what he himself thought of Samantha's journey to the Soviet Union. While video clips of Samantha's trip were on the list of news summaries recorded as having been shown on the White House's closed-circuit television, no records of whether the president watched the tapes have been kept, according to the Ronald Reagan Presidential Library. But Reagan's advisers clearly felt a certain degree of threat in the extraordinary amount of press coverage Samantha's trip had received—so much so that they considered arranging for President Reagan to receive a letter from a nine-year-old Soviet Jewish boy in hopes of undermining the Soviets, who, they were sure, were trying to undermine the Americans.

I'd like to think that President Reagan—whose memorial site at the library reads, "I know in my heart that man is good, that what is right will always eventually triumph and there is purpose and worth to each and every life"—did indeed show interest in Samantha's trip to the Soviet Union. After all, he had been captivated by Secretary of State George Shultz's trip to China just a few months prior and brought up his desire to travel to China and the Soviet Union during their February 1983 meeting. On July 11, when Sam was in Artek, Reagan sent a handwritten letter to Yuri Andropov that was declassified a decade later: "You and I share an enormous responsibility for the preservation of stability in the world. . . . [T]o do so will require a more active level of exchange than we have heretofore been able to establish." Acknowledging that their predecessors had "made better progress" when their communications had been "private and candid," he invited Andropov to engage in secret correspondence.

In January 1984, Reagan met with Suzanne Massie, a scholar of Russian history and culture, who helped him better understand the history of Russia and its people. She taught him the phrase *Doveryai, no proveryai* (Trust but verify), a saying that Reagan used frequently during his summits with Mikhail Gorbachev.

PART III

WELCOME HOME!

MAY 2013, BOOTHBAY, MAINE

In the spring of 2013, in Jane's attic, I picked up a large stuffed rabbit from among the pile of toys on the floor. With its unusually short arms, it looked strangely familiar. "I've seen him before," I said to Jane. I quickly flipped through the pages of my old scrapbook until I saw a picture of Samantha with that very rabbit. A handmade toy, it was a gift from one of the friendship clubs in Leningrad, the caption said.

"After our first visit to the Soviet Union, a friend of mine came to visit," Jane said. "I took her upstairs to show her the stuffed animals that Sam had received as gifts. . . . She looked at the animals, was sort of thoughtful, and then said, 'You know, I just don't think of the Soviets as having stuffed animals for their children.'"

19

WELCOME HOME, SAMANTHA!

JULY 1983, MANCHESTER, MAINE

In Richmond, Virginia, Sam's Pa was running from one room to the other, setting the VHS players to record coverage of his granddaughter's grand adventure to the Soviet Union. He and Grannie were beyond proud of Sam. In Manchester, Maine, Nonnie and Sam's cousin Tyler were housesitting and taking care of Sam's dog Kim and answering the phone. During their trip, the phone rang only three or four times a day, but now that their July 22 arrival was approaching, it was needing attention every ten minutes. They were being inundated with interview requests: ABC, NBC, and CBS were vying for the first interview with Sam after her trip and were all asking the same questions: "What time is the plane coming in? What airline? What's the flight number? Are there reporters in the house?"

"I don't know how Arthur did it," Nonnie lamented. Earlier in the week, she had given her own interview to the *Washington Post* and the *New York Times*. In response to those criticizing Samantha's trip, she said, "I think you get bad reactions to even a good piece of cake. It's their prerogative if they have bad things in their background that won't let them accept an endeavor to make friends. Ninety-nine percent of the letters urged her to go."

On July 22, the *Telegraph* newspaper reported that Transport Canada had tried to arrange free tickets for Samantha and her family to watch the

National League Baseball game on the way home from the trip. Expos president John McHale, the *Telegraph* revealed, turned down the request out of fear that the media would bother regular season ticket holders, who had a right to see the game undisturbed. Had Jane and Arthur known of the proposal, they would have nipped it in the bud—by then they were so tired, they just wanted to get home. To the reporters who waited for them in the Montreal airport, Sam said she was convinced that the Soviet people "want no harm to the world, just like I don't." But, she added, "I'd rather live in my home country." They then got into the limo provided by the Soviet consulate and headed to the hotel to catch up on sleep before their flight to Boston.

By the time they got to Boston, Sam was almost in tears, tired, and unwilling to engage with the reporters. "I don't think Samantha really wants to talk," Arthur explained. "I'm sorry but she needs a few days off from the crush." He said he hoped that the trip had some positive benefit. "There must be some reason for this interest here and in the Soviet Union." There were no immediate plans to write any more letters, he added.

In Augusta, a crowd of over three hundred people packed the tiny airport lobby, with more peering through the fences around the runway when the Smiths' Bar Harbor flight landed at 3:30 p.m. on Friday. Sam, wearing a green shirt and lavender pants, was a little more upbeat by the time their plane touched down in Maine, especially when she saw Nonnie at the bottom of the plane steps. She shrieked and ran into her arms.

After a red-carpet welcome, which included a reading of the letter from Senator William Cohen, they were escorted to an antique black-and-maroon Rolls-Royce limousine volunteered by a local business for the five-mile ride home. When asked whether she would do it again, tired Sam managed only a quiet yes.

"We won't miss the permanent entourage of the press," commented Arthur when the family arrived at their house on Worthing Road. "The press was part of our baggage."

By the front door, Sam paused and tapped her heels together, imitating Dorothy from *The Wizard of Oz*: "There is no place like home!"

The next morning, Saturday, July 23, Jane and Arthur welcomed *Kennebec Journal* reporter Jack Weible, who had first broken the news of

Sam's letter to Andropov back in April. His was going to be the very first story after their return to the United States. They had cancelled their trip to New York for the morning TV shows as well as all other interviews except Sam's appearance on *The Tonight Show Starring Johnny Carson* at the end of the following week.

"We want to try to relax and behave normally for a while," Jane said.

"We have to start saying no to interviews or we'll drop dead. Sam really needs to get her batteries recharged," said Arthur.

They agreed that they owed it to the public to let them see the girl who had written to Andropov. "At the same time," Arthur said, "we would like things to let up a bit."

On the table, in neatly stacked piles, lay the letters that came for Sam while they were gone. Some were from teachers who wanted her to share her experiences with their classrooms. Some were pen pal requests. Different peace movement causes had written as well. Their future involvement with the organizations, Jane and Arthur agreed, would depend on Sam. "We are not totally opposed to identification between Samantha Smith and world peace." There was an offer from the publisher of a travel journal who wanted to pay expenses for a Soviet child and his parents to spend two weeks with the Smiths next summer. Jane and Arthur said they would consider the offer. Only a handful of the letters were negative: some scolded Samantha for wearing a Communist uniform in Artek; others chastised her for writing in the first place. The recent issue of the *Kennebec Journal* had published two letters on Samantha, one suggesting that she "stay home and play with dolls, rather than promote peace," the other pleading for "an end to the envious sniping that has been going on."

Former secretary of state Dean Rusk, who had served under both the John F. Kennedy and the Lyndon B. Johnson administrations, also wrote to Sam: "The purpose of this note is to simply say that I was enchanted by the way you handled yourself on that extraordinary visit. You gave the Russians a chance to see an attractive, natural and unpretentious young American and therefore made a significant contribution towards understanding between the peoples of our two countries."

Earlier in the morning, Sam and Lynn had gone to see *Staying Alive* with John Travolta and now were giggling upstairs as Jane and Arthur unpacked the gifts. The large samovar from Andropov and the tea set got a lot of "oohs" and "ahhs" on their back porch. As Weible took notes, Arthur shared how the housing shortages were "not taboo for discussion" among the Soviets. He also mentioned the candid comments on the futility of the arms race by the first woman cosmonaut, Tereshkova. Jane was struck by the devastation imposed on the Soviet Union during World War II.

"So many of the kids Sam met had grandparents who fought or died in World War II," she said. "The people in the Soviet Union love children," she added, "and are very affectionate."

"Sam tried her darnedest to be polite," Arthur shared. "Despite some sporadic fatigue," he said, "she enjoyed the trip." He was particularly struck, he said, by her "native enthusiasm," which he hadn't known she had.

That day, Manchester held its annual Old Manchester Day parade with Sam as its guest of honor. Hundreds of cars lined the mile-long parade route on that sunny morning. There were Brownie and Boy Scout troops, a flatbed trailer with eight members of the Manchester Community Church in light blue robes singing hymns, and clowns carrying a banner that read, "Welcome Home Samantha."

"With camera toting spectators clumped in lawn chairs and on tailgates to glimpse the winsome veteran of the world of high diplomacy," as the *Lewiston Daily Sun* reporter described the scene, the attendance was a record since the parade's inception in 1977.

"Hi Sam!" echoed from the blue pickup truck that carried Sam's softball teammates, the Malacites. They were a few vehicles behind the baby-blue 1965 Mustang that carried Sam and her parents. Sam, dressed in a bright green top, white print skirt, and white knee socks, waved from her car-top perch and tossed out candy.

On stage, Governor Joseph E. Brennan congratulated Sam as the army of photographers clicked away and television crews moved to catch her every smile.

"We are proud of the way you have conducted yourself under the lights of the television cameras," the governor said. "Samantha has captured the hearts of people around the world, with her grace, with charm, and with a simple but elegant message of peace."

Sam climbed up on a box next to the microphone. "Thanks, an awful lot. I'm awful glad to be home," she said.

One of the town officials handed her the ceremonial key to the town. "I must be dreaming," Sam said.

The following week, on Thursday, July 28, Sam was in Los Angeles for her second appearance on *The Tonight Show*. She sat up in the chair next to the host, this time making sure her legs didn't dangle.

After learning that in Moscow the airport and planes were pretty much the same as in the United States and that Sam wasn't crazy about some of the Russian food, though she did enjoy chicken Kiev, Johnny Carson asked about Moscow's metro stations.

"Do they actually have chandeliers hanging in the subways?"

"Yes, they do," Sam answered and described the intricate mosaics and paintings inside the Moscow underground.

"I wonder how long that would last in New York," joked Carson to the audience's great delight. "We have paintings in New York subway also—#5 aerosol can."

Although they made a valiant effort to keep the reporters at bay for the first two weeks after they returned from the Soviet Union, by the end of August, Sam had made nine TV appearances. Nonnie, very proud of her granddaughter, kept adding to the list she typed up on Arthur's typewriter:

7/28/83—Tonight Show w/J. Carson
8/15/83—The Donahue Show (Chicago)
8/15/83—Nightline, live remote from Chicago, w/Hugh Downs

There she noted the question Sam was asked—"Didn't they just show you the best?"—alongside her granddaughter's response: "Well, if I brought a new friend to my house, I wouldn't show them my messed-up closet or take them down to our trashy basement."

8/15/83—Eyewitness News, local Chicago affiliate
8/23/83—Good afternoon, Detroit, WXYZ Detroit talkshow
8/23/83—PBS Latenight w/ D. Wholey, WTVS Detroit

August
- *Evening PM Magazine, Boston, producer: V. Whitmore*
- *KRO, Dutch National TV, w/ Simon Mammelburg*
- *Maine Public Service spot: Dept. of Fish and Wildlife*

A couple of weeks later, the Smiths received a phone call from Al Burton, a Los Angeles–based television producer, who called to say that Sam had a great future in television and offered his help. Sam was very excited. Once again, Arthur and Jane had a difficult decision to make: any long-term commitments now meant Sam might have to miss school.

"I don't think it's a parent's business to shield their children from good experiences," was Arthur's take on it. "She enjoys this, she meets people. And she's capable. That is a gift she has. I'm not about to deny her that experience." They agreed to have Burton explore the possibilities for her.

20

"LOOK AROUND AND SEE ONLY FRIENDS"

SEPTEMBER 1983, MANCHESTER, MAINE / DECEMBER 1983, KOBE, JAPAN

After Samantha's family returned to Manchester, news coverage in the Soviet Union stopped, so I went about the last days of that summer spending time with friends, playing in the yard of the Sleeping Skyscraper. On my eighth birthday, September 1, 1983, I started second grade. I wore a white apron on top of my brown school uniform dress and carried a bouquet of asters for Nina Mikhailovna. I didn't know that on the morning of my eighth birthday, we came very close to the brink of war.

That morning, Korean Airlines (KAL) Flight 007, on its last leg from New York to Seoul via Anchorage, Alaska, entered Soviet airspace and crossed over the Kamchatka Peninsula, the site of many top-secret Soviet military installations. The Soviets sent two fighter planes to intercept the plane. After the KAL flight didn't respond, the Soviets assumed it was a spy plane camouflaged as a passenger jet and fired a heat-seeking missile to destroy it. All 269 passengers and crew members were killed instantly. The Soviet government's failure to acknowledge right away that it had shot down the passenger jet by mistake outraged the West. In the United States, Ronald Reagan called the event a massacre. The relations between the two countries hit a new low.

In Maine, Sam was starting sixth grade at Manchester Elementary. On September 5, 1983, the Smiths watched Reagan's speech on the shooting down of KAL 007.

> *Hello, Americans. I'm coming before you tonight about the Korean airline massacre, the attack by the Soviet Union against the 269 innocent men, women, and children aboard an unarmed Korean passenger plane. This crime against humanity must never be forgotten, here or throughout the world. Our prayers tonight are with the victims and their families in their time of terrible grief. . . . There was no justification, either legal or moral, for what the Soviets did.*

"Gosh, why would they do such a stupid thing?" Sam asked, as the three of them watched the address. They were stunned by the news, not sure how something like that could have happened.

The next day, reporters were at Manchester Elementary School to take pictures and ask for Sam's reaction.

"We should just be talking," she said. "If the war starts, I would write again to Andropov, because he promised me he would never start a war with our country. I'm worried about the war, but I still trust them."

They called Arthur and Jane at home, asking for their thoughts on the incident.

"We all were upset, and we didn't really understand how that could possibly happen. But it points up even stronger the original inquiry that Samantha made—that she was worried about the threat of war. It's strong evidence that we can't go on this way."

Arthur was not sure why people wanted Sam's opinion on the incident. "Many people don't realize that an eleven-year-old doesn't sit around and discuss politics," he said.

"We are not Soviet experts in anything except our trip," added Jane. "We mostly met children on our trip. But this incident is the best example you could find to continue to find solutions to international problems. That's what Samantha's letter was all about."

Then the phones stopped ringing, and they thought that their lives just might go back to normal.

The beginning of that school year was tough for Sam. Kids who hadn't paid her much attention before now wanted to be her friends. Others called her a Communist. By the end of September, Sam was having a difficult time in all her classes and was flunking science: "2 failing quizzes and poor experiment," Jane wrote in her notes after a meeting with Sam's teachers on September 28, 1983. Sam was never good in science, and math wasn't her strong point either. Jane remembered how back in Amity, she was very frustrated when Sam couldn't memorize her addition and subtraction tables. They just wouldn't stick. Yet she had managed to keep up with the others once she started school—until now. It looked like she was going to fail the class. The two of them reviewed for the next science unit together, Sam studying for what seemed like hours, but then she got 68 percent on her test. On her next science quiz, she got 57 percent. They didn't know what they were doing wrong. Was everything getting boring after such a whirlwind trip? Were their expectations too high? Were the teachers being too hard on her because of all the news coverage? Or maybe they didn't like her idea of friendship with the Soviets? Maybe Sam just wanted to be like everyone else?

"Don't talk about your trip unless asked," Arthur advised—in hopes that it would help. But, of course, that was wishful thinking. With the worldwide coverage all summer and her appearances on *The Tonight Show*, not talking about it didn't really do any good.

Then, in December, about three months after the KAL incident, *The Today Show*, cohosted by Bryant Gumbel, called: they wanted to invite Sam to New York to interview US Arms Control Agency director Kenneth Adelman. Sam interviewed Adelman, who was in Washington, DC, from *The Today Show*'s New York studio. She was joined by two other children: Julia Duchrow, twelve, in Frankfurt, West Germany, and Anatol Sleeman, eight, in London, England.

"Why do we appear to spend more money building bombs than we do trying to help the poor or trying to talk at the peace talks?" Sam asked in her interview.

"I think what we want to do, Samantha, is spend money both for safety, to preserve our freedom, and to help our poor," answered Adelman.

"It is a tremendous value to help people in need, but it's also a tremendous value to keep ourselves free and safe and out of war."

Then came an invitation to Japan—for Sam to speak at the Children's International Symposium for the 21st Century in Kobe. "It may surprise you to know you have become quite well known in Japan," wrote the hosts of the upcoming International Exposition, Tsukuba Japan 1985. The Japanese newspapers dubbed Sam the "Angel of Peace."

Jane traveled with Sam, leaving Arthur behind to celebrate Christmas with his family. At the Portland airport, the reporters asked Sam about missing Christmas.

"Well, it's OK. I mean, I'm going to Japan," Sam replied.

On their ten-day trip, Sam was joining four young reporters and editors of a children's news organization called The Children's Express: Lisa Clampitt, nineteen; Felicia Kornbluh, seventeen; Steven Naplan, thirteen; and Rebecca Walkowitz, thirteen. They flew to New York and then on to Tokyo, and on Saturday, December 24, they were in Kyoto, where their hosts planned a visit for them to the Kiymizu Temple, the Nijo Castle, and the Heian Shrine and its gardens. Everywhere they went, people recognized Sam.

Felicia Kornbluh had come to Japan with a heavy heart: she carried a sense of guilt over the atomic bombs the United States had dropped on Hiroshima and Nagasaki during World War II. But then, at one of the department stores that they toured, she witnessed the media go crazy over Samantha: "Samantha, over here! Samantha, turn to us! Samantha, smile for us! Thank you for coming to Japan!" Sam was totally embraced by the Japanese. Felicia felt Sam represented what was good about America. It was a healing moment, Felicia thought. She exhaled.

On Christmas Day, they arrived in Kobe, where the Children's International Symposium for the 21st Century was being held. The next day, Sam gave her speech, "Look Around and See Only Friends," which she cowrote with Arthur and Al Burton. Wearing a blazer and plaid skirt, she walked up to the microphone.

I have to begin with an apology. My father helped me with my speech and look—I discovered that he doesn't know a single word of Japanese! Luckily, I have learned some of your language. Since I got here, I have been trying to learn as much as possible. So let me begin by saying Nihon no minasan Konnichiwa (Hello everybody in Japan).

I think maybe you should know something about me and the way I live back home. I was born in northern Maine, and we lived at the edge of the wilderness for most of my life. We even had bears and bobcats and moose visiting our backyard. Now I live in a town called Manchester, Maine. It is a small, country town. The number of people in town is about 2,000. I probably saw more people than that at the airport here. Like most kids eleven years old, I'm in the sixth grade and the subjects I study are English, reading, math, science, and social studies. Until last April, I had never traveled outside the eastern United States, I had never even heard of sushi!

Then, because I had written a letter to Yuri Andropov, I found myself in Moscow, Leningrad, and at a beautiful camp on the Black Sea near Yalta. I was on airplanes that took me over many foreign countries. After my trip to Russia—which actually should be called the Soviet Union—I came back to the same school and the same teachers and the same kids in Manchester, Maine. I didn't think I had changed at all, but, boy, had they changed!

Well, they were all asking questions like they had never asked before: What was the Soviet Union like? What were the kids like over there? How was the food? I discovered that my trip had made us all aware of parts of the world and people of the world that none of us had ever paid much attention to before.

And now I'll admit that I discovered I had changed, too. I don't feel as nervous in front of new people anymore. And I don't worry so much about understanding how people act in other lands. If I could bring the people of Maine here, you'd see that they're peaceful and easy to get along with. And I discovered that I grew up a lot this year.

But, today, we are not here to look back on the summer or to look backward at all. We are here to look ahead. I spent the last several weeks picturing myself in the year 2001 and thought of all the things that I would like the world to be eighteen years from today.

First of all, I don't want to have these freckles anymore, and I want this tooth straightened, and I hope I like the idea of being almost thirty. Maybe it's because I have traveled a lot and maybe it's because I've met so many wonderful people who look a little different from the way I look—maybe their skin, or their eyes, or their language is not like mine—but I can picture them becoming my best friends. . . . Maybe it's because of these things that I think the year 2001 and the years that follow are going to be just great.

When I close my eyes and think about the future, this is what I see. I see a computer and stored in that computer is information on exactly how much food there is in the world. It tells where there are large crops. It tells where the wheat supply is good for that year, and also about the crops of corn and rice and potatoes, and it won't forget the beef and poultry and fish.

This computer will also show where the people are who don't have enough food. By the year 2001, the computer can also tell us where the ships and the airplanes are that can take the food from where it is directly to the people who need it.

In my computer of the year 2001, it also says where the wood for houses and the steel and concrete for building can be found, and it shows where the work are for the building [sic] the new houses and roads and hospitals and schools and factories.

And when I close my eyes, guess what? I know how to work that computer and match up all of the things that will be needed for the people who will need them. And soon we will know how to move one to the other regardless of what country they're in or what borders have to be crossed.

My computer of 2001 will transfer good food, good shelter, and good clothing to the people who need them, and all of it will come from places and countries where these things are plentiful so that it won't hurt what my teacher explains is "the balance of trade."

In my 2001, there's an abundance of everything, and lots of ways to harvest it and transport it to people in need.

By the way, my computer is made up of microchips and wires and electric gismos from probably 158 different countries. It's a very friendly international computer, and I hope you'll join me in 2001, to help push all the buttons.

Next, I would like to share with you a wish not for 2001, but for this year 1984, the new year.

What I wish for is something I'll call the International Grand-daughter Exchange. I guess if I were a boy, I'd call it the International Grandson Exchange. But I'm not a boy, so I'll stick with granddaughter. The International Granddaughter Exchange would have the highest political leaders in nations all over the world sending their granddaughters or nieces—(or, okay, grandsons and nephews)—to live with families of opposite nations. Soviet leaders' granddaughters would spend two weeks in America. American leaders' granddaughters would spend two weeks in the Soviet Union. And, wherever possible, granddaughters of other opposing countries would exchange visits and we would have better understanding all over the world.

And now I will try my wish in Japanese: Sekaiju ni heiwa ga kimasu yo mi (I wish for world peace and understanding).

Last summer, I had the amazing chance to visit the beautiful and awesome Soviet Union. I loved making friends with those girls and boys, and I think they enjoyed meeting an American kid. Let's keep doing it! Let's find a way to get some of those girls and boys to visit Japan, and America, and China, and Peru. And let's find a way for you to visit Soviet kids and American kids, kids who can't speak a word of Japanese—even kids who drive in American cars.

If we start with an International Granddaughter Exchange and keep expanding it and expanding it, then the year 2001 can be the year when all of us can look around and see only friends, no opposite nations, no enemies, and no bombs.

My grandparents are not important political leaders. In fact, one grandfather of mine was a doctor and one is a retired minister. But I've had the privilege of being an international granddaughter and let me tell you that it is one terrific experience.

We have started our exciting trip to the year 2001. I've told you two of my favorite visions: the far-off vision of a computer to help deliver the world's abundance to the world's needy, and a closer vision, the International Granddaughter Exchange.

My father, who is back in Maine, didn't help with the end of my speech, so he'll probably be surprised when I say, why don't you all come back home with me and meet my friends there!

Thank you for your attention. Domo arigato gozai mashita.

21

SAMANTHA SMITH GOES TO WASHINGTON

JANUARY–FEBRUARY 1984, WASHINGTON, DC, MASSACHUSETTS, SOUTH CAROLINA, FLORIDA, AND CALIFORNIA

When Jane and Sam returned from Japan, they learned that plans for yet another adventure had been set in motion. Al Burton, who had been exploring possibilities for Sam in TV, had heard that the Disney Channel was looking for a new TV project. Then a brand-new cable channel that had premiered the same month Sam received Yuri Andropov's response, the Disney Channel focused on projects for young people. When its founding president Jim Jimirro heard that Sam's claim to fame was talking to a world leader, the idea came to him "within six seconds": she could interview all the presidential candidates for the upcoming 1984 election. And when the network president comes up with an idea, "it will get made and put on the air," Arnold Shapiro, who was to become the new show's producer, shared years later. With "Al supplying the talent, [and] Jim . . . supplying the network," it was a very successful partnership. Since the presidential interviews needed a nonfiction format, Shapiro, a documentary producer and Burton's close friend, who was already producing *Wish upon a Star* for the Disney Channel, was just the man for the job. It was agreed that Arnold Shapiro Productions would produce the special, with Shapiro as the executive producer and Jean O'Neill as the producer.

The filming took Sam and Arthur, who by then had stopped taking on teaching assignments at the university, to Washington, DC, Massachusetts, South Carolina, Florida, and California at the start of 1984. The show's producer, Jean O'Neill, worked closely with Sam on the question selection for the interviews. Since they wanted to create a program that families could watch together, to show the candidates as people and not just as politicians, they tried to balance the political questions with topics kids might really be interested in—like "the time you ran away from home" or "did you get into trouble as a kid," the sorts of things that Sam wanted to ask. Years later, O'Neill would remember that Sam had a strong presence, a great work ethic, and "an excellent sense as to what people might like to know."

"Most people know me as the girl who went to Russia, but now I am going to Washington," Sam said as she introduced herself while walking toward the camera in the snowy suburbs of Washington, DC, where the filming started in January 1984.

Almost as soon as they started filming, PBS's *Inside Story* decided to follow Sam and her crew, putting extra pressure on Sam, as she would have no opportunities to fix her mistakes. All the wraparounds—the on-camera introductions and closings, which PBS was particularly keen on shooting—would have to be nailed the first time.

Years later, O'Neill remembered how the night before the shoot, she was trying to rehearse with Sam, and she was just fooling around, saying she knew her copy. Yet Jean hadn't seen her learning lines at all, so she asked Sam to recite the lines for her. Sam delivered her lines "machine gun fast, without pauses or inflection. But she didn't miss a word."

The next day, when they set up across the street from the White House, the PBS crew was already there. Jean was nervous, as Sam had never really rehearsed with the right delivery.

With the White House in the background, Sam started. "The White House, the most famous house in America and the home of our president. Quite a few people are trying to get your vote so that they can start living here next year. As a special correspondent for the Disney Channel, I'm going to track down and interview as many of the presidential candidates as I can." She didn't miss anything.

The closing scene had an added challenge: halfway through, Sam had to do a head turn and continue her speech looking at a different camera.

"Even professional newscasters sometimes mess up the timing," O'Neill remembered, "but [Sam's] first take was perfect—every word, inflection, even the head turn. She was a natural."

Their first stop was Boston, Massachusetts, where Sam was to interview former Florida governor Reubin Askew, who was on his way home from the New Hampshire debate. Sam, dressed up to look older and more like a professional, wore a skirt and a blazer, with a tie.

"I do babysitting. What did you do to earn money when you were a kid?" was Sam's first question.

Askew shared about his childhood in Oklahoma and an aunt who used to pay him in nickels and pennies for swatting flies around the house. He also shined shoes, had a paper route, and worked in a grocery store. Sam also asked how Governor Askew felt about "inviting Soviets over here to talk about peace." Askew said he saw no reason why "this country and the Soviet Union can't get together and seek out more commonality of interest."

Two days later, in New Hampshire, Sam sat down with George McGovern.

"You're the only candidate who says that we can cut the military budget and still feel safe. Why is that?" Sam asked.

McGovern, an old-school bomber pilot from World War II, replied that he would never advocate for the policy if he "thought that [his] recommendations were cutting into anything that we need[ed] for defense." But, he noted, there were "hundreds of millions of dollars in cost overruns" by the Pentagon, which purchased US weapons systems. "See if I can illustrate it for you," McGovern said. "You can go to your town in Manchester, Maine, and buy a hammer in a hardware store for about six bucks, maybe seven, maybe five, but somewhere in that range. Pentagon buys that hammer custom made, and they pay about $400 on the average, for every hammer that they have in their defense department. Why? What are they pounding over there that is so precious that they have to pound it with a $400 hammer?"

Sam's eyes grew big at the price of the custom-made hammer.

"Well, that wouldn't be so bad; we can probably get away with wasting $400 on a hammer," continued McGovern. "But when they use the same methods to buy airplanes, and tanks and ships, we end up spending tens of billions of dollars more than is necessary; that's bad."

Next stop was the campaign headquarters of the South Carolina senator Ernest Hollings, whom Sam asked, "Why aren't you thinking to get a woman or a minority to be your running mate?"

Hollings replied that he had indeed suggested as much over a year and half ago to Chuck Manatt, the Democratic Party chairman, but was told that "we weren't ready." "I said we were," Hollings continued. "In fact, looking to the strengths of our party, rather than looking geographically, we could get a woman or a minority or perhaps both, and I mentioned Barbara Jordan at the time."

"What advice would you give me if I wanted to be a politician?"

Hollings suggested that her first priority should be studying English, so that she knew "how to communicate and express" herself, followed by learning history and involving herself "with current affairs." "It's the most interesting endeavor I know," he concluded.

Sam was really engaged with the interviews, enjoying herself immensely. There was only one time when she was genuinely nervous during the filming. At Howard University, she was slated to interview Reverend Jesse Jackson. Her earlier interviews were held in relatively low-key settings, but the ballroom at Howard University, where Arthur, Sam, and the crew waited and waited for Jackson to arrive, was cavernous and dark. Being only the second Black presidential candidate of a major party, Jackson had Secret Service men "in suits and tiny headsets, backs to the wall, next to each doorway, eyes focused on the doors across the rooms," Jean O'Neill remembered. There were also a lot of staff members and press.

When Jackson walked in, he must have sensed Sam's nervousness because he sat down, took her hands in his, and told her to take deep breaths. She did. It seemed to work, and she relaxed and asked her first question.

"If you were to pick three words to describe yourself, what would they be?"

"Is the whole interview going to be this way?" Jackson laughed.

After some thought, he chose the words "concern, commitment, discipline."

Within a few minutes, Jackson was the one asking questions.

"What made you think that your letter would get through to Andropov?"

"I don't know," Sam said. "I thought if it happened with Queen Elizabeth, it might as well happen with Andropov."

"When you were growing up, did you ever write Santa Claus?"

"No," Sam answered, laughing.

"You never tried that? But you did write to Andropov and you got your response? Has that done anything for your confidence? Your ability to kind of make things happen?"

"Well, I'm not as shy anymore."

"See, the reason I'm asking is that most people, young people and adults, don't have enough self-confidence to try to make something happen. Most people in the world feel the same way you feel about nuclear destruction, and yet they don't have that little something you had to write that letter. I hope you maintain that property in your life as long as you live."

"Thank you very much!" Sam was charmed by his kind comments. Jackson became her favorite.

They then flew to Los Angeles, where Sam was scheduled to interview Senator Alan Cranston. Unfortunately, a mishap with the LA airport baggage compartment left Sam's bag completely destroyed and her without her wardrobe. Sam took the incident in stride: Jean had to take her shopping, and shopping in LA sounded like fun.

"If you became president, would you stop building nuclear bombs?" Sam asked Senator Cranston.

"This is an interest I share very deeply with you, and I admire the work you've done about the nuclear arms race," said Cranston.

If I'm elected president, the day I take the oath of office, on January 20, 1985, I will announce that the United States will not test or deploy any more nuclear weapons as long as the Soviets don't. That won't take any negotiating, we'd just announce it. If they tested or deployed, we would know it, and then we could do whatever was necessary. I'd do another thing that day—I would get in touch with the Soviet leader and say, "Let's get together at the earliest possible moment to reach an agreement on stopping producing nuclear bombs, nuclear weapons and start talking about how we reduce the stockpiles, reduce the targeting, reduce the dangers, reduce the cost." We have to abolish these weapons from the face of God's Earth, and if we don't, sooner or later, even though we and the Soviets don't intend it or want it, I believe we will land in the nuclear war that will wipe out the whole human race. It will certainly destroy our country and destroy the Soviet country.

On returning to Washington, DC, Sam met with Senator John Glenn. With Glenn, a former astronaut, Sam talked about the importance of education and increasing teacher pay. "So many kids really don't like school much. What are you going to do about that—trying to make them happier going to school?" she asked Glenn.

Glenn tried to emphasize the importance of education and compared the number of days a US schoolchild spends in school to that of students in other countries. "The average young person in this country goes to school about 185 days each year, and we think that's a lot of work, and it is, but do we know that in Europe and most of the other countries, kids are in school 210 to 220 days a year? And in Japan, kids go to school 240 days a year. They have half-day on Saturday every week."

Sam squirmed at the idea.

They stayed an extra two days in DC in hopes of meeting with Gary Hart and Walter Mondale. But neither of the two, nor the incumbent President Reagan, could meet with her. It wasn't for the lack of trying, Arnold Shapiro recalled three decades later. Perhaps the "two front-runners didn't want to take the time to sit down with a child interviewer (since that in itself was a first)," but he thought their staffs most likely had made the decision, not the candidates themselves. Jean O'Neill thought that the front-runners "had less to gain and more to lose by agreeing to be interviewed by a kid for something that would air on what was then a brand-new network with relatively few viewers."

Samantha Smith Goes to Washington: Campaign '84, aptly named after a classic movie, was heavily promoted by Disney. This was the first time that the preteen appeared on national television, starring in her own cable network special, interviewing presidential candidates—all by herself. It debuted at 6:00 p.m. on Sunday, February 19, and was shown on five other dates later in the month.

"I'm sorry that not all the candidates agreed to be interviewed, but I'd like to thank the ones who did," Sam said. "For me, it's been terrific. I learned a lot about these men and their ideas, and I hope you have too. But whether you support one of the candidates I talked to or someone else, remember, if you're old enough, please, vote. And although kids my age can't vote, we can talk to our parents and tell them what we think. And maybe they'll listen. This is Samantha Smith in Washington."

That month Sam promoted the upcoming special on *The Today Show*. Bryant Gumbel started his interview with a question about Sam's reaction to the passing of Yuri Andropov, who had died a few days earlier, on February 9, 1984.

"A reporter called me at six o'clock in the morning," Sam said, "and told me that Yuri Andropov had died, and it really was a horrible shock. I was really sad about that."

Gumbel then asked about her presidential interviews and wanted to know whether she had developed a favorite.

"Yeah," Sam replied.

"Do you want to share?"

"No," Sam said.

"You've learned that already," laughed Gumbel.

"So real quick," he continued, "you went to the Soviet Union on the mission of peace, you went to Japan to the Children's Symposium on Science and Technology, you've interviewed the Democratic candidates— are you going to continue to be kind of a public person?"

"I don't know," Sam shrugged her shoulders. "It depends on what happens next."

"You've already covered a lot of ground for eleven years," said Gumbel. "Samantha, good luck!"

"Thank you!"

The remainder of 1984 was a whirlwind. What the Smiths had initially thought would be just fifteen minutes of fame didn't seem to end. The offers for Sam kept pouring in. On April 25, 1984, on the first anniversary of Andropov's reply, the *News and Courier* announced the publication by Little, Brown and Company of *The Journey to the Soviet Union* by Samantha Smith, detailing her trip.

"Actually, the whole thing started when I asked my mother if there was going to be a war," Sam stated, opening her reportage on her correspondence with the Soviet leader and her trip to the Soviet Union. Alongside pictures of her with Andropov's response and that of her reading yet another newspaper about her correspondence with the Soviet leader, there were photographs the Smiths received from the Soviet TASS news agency of Sam touring Red Square, meeting Valentina Tereshkova in Moscow, and engaging with the Soviet campers in Artek.

"Sometimes I still worry that the next day will be the last day of the Earth. But with more people thinking about the problems of the world, I hope that someday soon we will find the way to world peace. Maybe someone will show us the way."

In the foreword, famous child psychologist Lee Salk wrote, "Samantha has become a symbol of hope to all children. Her simple question, supported by loving parents, led to greater human understanding, and has shown us the power of a child in lessening the tensions between two world powers."

In the fall of 1984, Al Burton, who was also an executive producer for the new TV series *Charles in Charge*, offered Sam a guest appearance on its sixth episode, "Slumber Party." Sam joined triple-medal-winning Olympic gymnast Julianne McNamara in a guest appearance and played one of the kids that Scott Baio's character was stuck babysitting. Her role was small, and she had only a few lines, but she was genuinely amused by the rehearsals, which she described in her English assignment.

Doing rehearsal is really crazy. I mean you can hardly get through one scene in 45 minutes. The director, Alan was always saying, "Wait a minute, Allison. Move over. You're in Willie's picture." Or "No, Betsy, don't wear your jacket, just carry it." Then we'd go back and do that part all over again.

I kept having to do my, "Do I have to kiss you?" to Scott. It got to be real embarrassing.

But I lived through it all and taping went great and this episode will be on November 14, 1984.

In December 1984, Sam and Arthur traveled to Washington, DC, to visit the Soviet embassy school where Sam was given a tour by Ambassador Anatoly Dobrynin's granddaughter Ekaterina. Sam gave a little speech in front of two hundred children who went to the embassy school and joined them in singing "May There Always Be Sunshine" and "It's a Small World" and handed out toys from the *Get Along Gang* show. The news that night showed Sam and her friends, accompanied by Montgomery the Moose, by the gates of the Soviet embassy.

"What do you think you accomplished?" asked the reporters.

"Hope for peace at least between our children. Which I think we could probably do," Sam replied.

"What prompted you to do this?"

"Well, because it doesn't seem right now that Soviets and us are getting along very well, but I'd like to be friends at least with the Soviet children. Which we are."

When asked about the upcoming meeting between Secretary of State George Shultz and Soviet foreign minister Andrei Gromyko in Geneva to discuss arms control, Sam replied, "I think it's really great!"

"Do you hope to return to the Soviet Union sometime?"

"Hopefully. In the later years."

"Do you think you will be invited back for another visit?"

Sam wasn't sure how to answer.

"You are invited," said Ambassador Dobrynin's granddaughter.

The reporters then turned to the Soviet kids.

"Could you tell us what your reaction is to what's happening here?"

"We were very happy that Samantha was able to come here, and we would like to see her again here," said Irina Pavlova.

The reporters asked Irina whether she agreed with Samantha that there may be hope for the children, and if so, why.

"Yes, yes, we do," Irina said, adding, "If adults can't . . . I think the children can accomplish something useful . . . for better future and for peace, better relationship between our two countries."

22

LIME STREET

JANUARY–AUGUST 1985

Arthur's 1985 Day-Timer, which arrived at my home in a package from Jane in the spring of 2021, documented the schedule of Tempest Productions, as Arthur had by then, only half-jokingly, nicknamed the business of accompanying Sam on her engagements. Nineteen-eighty-five was shaping up to be another busy year.

One day early in the year, when Jane got home from work, Arthur told her that he had just talked with actor Robert Wagner. "Can you believe it?" Wagner called to ask whether Sam was interested in auditioning for the new TV series he was producing and starring in. The series, called *55 Lime Street*, was about globe-trotting insurance investigator James Greyson Culver, a character that combined Wagner's debonair style with his more domestic side. Culver was raising two daughters, Elizabeth and Margaret Ann. The series producers, Linda Bloodworth-Thomason and Harry Thomason, were looking for an actress to play the role of Elizabeth. Eight-year-old Maia Brewton, who had appeared in *Trapper John, M.D.*, *General Hospital*, and *Back to the Future*, was cast as Culver's daughter Margaret Ann. Elizabeth was described as "an old-fashioned kind of girl . . . who is polite, well-read, and aware of something in the world besides MTV." Hundreds of child actresses auditioned for the part, but none fit the bill exactly. Harry Thomason's brother Danny, an optometrist in Little Rock, Arkansas, had seen one of Sam's interviews and called Harry. "Here is a little girl you should look at."

Sam had no idea who Robert Wagner was, but she did have fond memories of her guest appearance on *Charles in Charge* and the camaraderie on set, so the prospect of acting again sounded like fun to her. When Linda Bloodworth-Thomason called to talk to Sam, Sam told her she couldn't come to an audition quite yet—their dog Kim had just had puppies and was proving a poor mother. Sam and Arthur were taking care of them while Kim ignored them.

"That is exactly what we wanted, that kind of quality," Bloodworth-Thomason commented years later.

Arthur and Sam flew to LA in February 1985. After her audition, Sam was almost in tears—she thought she had done terribly. When Linda told her that she had got the part, Sam couldn't believe it. The next day, they drove to meet with Wagner and do a reading for ABC.

"Be sure to look at her eyes," Wagner told the ABC executives as Sam walked up on stage; then he watched twenty of "ABC's top brass" tilt their heads to get a good look at her eyes during her performance. Years later, Wagner would remember how impressed he was with Sam's confidence. She didn't seem nervous at all during the audition, and the head of casting said, "She was magnificent, another Margaret O'Brien. A total natural."

The series pilot was going to be filmed in Washington, DC, Virginia, and Los Angeles, and Jane was going to take two weeks off work to fly with Sam. On February 26, 1985, the *Lewiston Daily Sun* announced, "Samantha Smith has a role in a TV series with Robert Wagner." It quoted Arthur saying this was "such a wonderful opportunity for Samantha to see and do things that [he and Jane were] certainly ready to follow her at this point." The article also mentioned that Sam would keep up with her homework with on-set tutors.

Thomas Schnurmacher of the *Montreal Gazette* was of a different opinion:

You remember Samantha? She's the bratty little kid who made headlines when she and Andropov became pen-pals. As you probably know by now, little Samantha will be working in Hollywood on an adventure series television pilot in which she would play the part of Robert

Wagner's daughter. This column tried to warn everyone that little Samantha and her daddy, college professor Arthur Smith, were not going to waste all the publicity she received on the glee clubs of Maine.

Arthur kept all the articles about Sam, both good and bad. A year earlier, right after their Soviet trip, Arthur and Jane had come under attack for pushing Sam to get involved in issues she knew nothing about. Charles Krauthammer, in his 1983 *Time* magazine article, quoted Sam's "They're just . . . almost . . . just like us" and also went after Jane, describing her as a "mother, who is no longer eleven but makes up for it in open-mindedness." After the Disney special came out, Krauthammer said in the *New Republic* that it was a way of "trivializing crucial political issues by paying attention to the opinions of children." With Sam "going to Hollywood," the remarks centered on the "exploitation of Samantha Smith."

Of course, Jane knew that Arthur saw these opportunities as a good thing for Sam. She got to meet new people, which she enjoyed, and got valuable experience, which he thought contributed to her education. "Anyone who is doing anything worthwhile is going to get a certain amount of criticism," he said. He was proud of Sam. She had surprised all of them during the Soviet trip and was amazing during the Disney Channel special, and he didn't want to deny her the opportunity of a possible career if she was interested. Plus, Sam was thriving, and seeing her happy made Arthur happy. For Arthur, who had been in low spirits after his heart attack and surgery, this adventure seemed to provide a new lease on life. Seeing the two of them discuss and plan things and pack for their trips made Jane smile.

Of course, as parents, they discussed the negatives. It seemed like almost every day they'd talk about whether this was moving too fast or whether they should just stop answering their phones. With the increased media attention that the Soviet trip and the Disney special brought, they also began to worry about Sam's safety, and Jane started to accompany her to the movies with friends. Sam didn't like that at all.

On May 3, Arthur noted in his Day-Timer, "Al Burton says rumor has it 55LS is on! So says ET [Entertainment Tonight]." When he broke the news of the show getting picked up to Sam, she started jumping up and down and screaming. *Lime Street*, as the show was soon known, was added to ABC's fall 1985 schedule at 9:00 p.m.—between a new cop drama series, *Hollywood Beat*, at 8:00 p.m. and the last season of *The Love Boat* at 10:00 p.m. *Lime Street* was set to air on September 21. Many predicted it would be the season's breakout hit.

On June 3, *People* magazine published an article about Sam and the show. Accompanied by pictures of her Universal Studios tour and one on set with Wagner, the article described Sam's journey from little ambassador to Hollywood actress and commented on her acting skills: "Samantha . . . has taken easily to her job. If she flubs a line, she grins a second, presses a hand to her face, then does another take—and usually does it perfectly."

By mid-summer Arthur's Day-Timer was punctuated by almost weekly interview requests. In June, there were *Education Week*, *Yankee Magazine*, and *TV Guide* interviews. Their flying schedule was getting too hectic: the long layovers, plane changes, and small airplanes on the last leg to Augusta were taking a toll on them. Now that it looked like they'd be doing the series for at least a year, they decided that renting an apartment in LA, near Columbia Studios, would be more prudent. Jane was worried about finding a job in LA, as one of them had to continue to work and the other needed to be with Sam on set. They planned to finalize their move before the start of the new 1985–1986 school year.

In July 1985, Arthur and Sam traveled to Virginia for the filming of *Lime Street*'s next episodes. The weather was hot and humid, but Sam was having fun, especially in the riding paddock, where she and her costar, Maia Brewton, would head between shots. Even though Maia was five years younger than Sam, she was a ton of fun, and Sam soon started to call Maia the little sister she'd never had. The crew knew that if they heard a thud somewhere in the house during the filming, it had to be the girls.

On set, Sam recited her lines with Maia or anyone else who had time. The girls got along very well with their costar, Wagner, who let them call him "RJ" and was excellent with kids. He was gracious and patient on set. Thirty years later, Wagner would remember a father-daughter dance scene they shot for the second episode. Elizabeth gets stood up by a popular boy in her class, and when her dad goes to comfort her and finds her crying, he asks her for the dance that the two had practiced earlier. Wagner counts, "One, two, three, slide," as the two of them dance to "This Moment in Time."

"You're going too fast," says Elizabeth.

"No, you're doing great, you're a natural," her dad replies.

"The scene still brings tears to my eyes," Wagner remembered years later.

When *Entertainment Tonight* asked Sam what was next, she kept things in perspective and said there was a lot she wanted to do with her life.

"I don't know what's going to happen to me," she said. "If people keep picking me up for other shows . . . I might wind up being an actress after all. But if things don't really happen after this show, I might end up being a veterinarian, or a hair stylist, or makeup artist, or I don't know."

Having finished the second episode, Arthur and Sam were back home on Sunday, August 4, 1985, not yet sure when the filming at their next location, London, would commence. The next weekend, Jane went camping with friends on the shore of Attean Pond. But the call to London came earlier than expected, with Sam and Arthur's departure set for Sunday, August 11. With no cellphones in 1985, there was no way for Jane to learn of the change in plans. For the first time since the routine of their frequent departures had set in two years before, Jane was camping and didn't get to help Arthur and Sam pack or say a proper good-bye.

They called home several times from London, first complaining of jet lag and detailing the first days of filming. The long hours tired Arthur out. "Call 6:15 AM," he wrote in his Day-Timer on Wednesday, August 14. "A long, hard day beginning at the tennis courts—all through the afternoon scenes with RJ—finished at 4:30PM." He met with the director, requesting no more long hours. Then there was a five-day break, which they filled with sightseeing. They saw Buckingham Palace, the British Museum, and Piccadilly Circus. They went to see *Starlight Express*, and Sam joined Maia and her dad Barney on a trip to Stratford, while Arthur spent a day in London and visited Boss and Co. to look at their fine shotguns. Arthur also took Sam to Harrods and Kings Road, where he tried to persuade her to buy a leather jacket in which she, to his surprise, had zero interest. "Must have looked at a thousand of them. Walked 6–7 miles," he wrote on August 17. The last couple of days were tiring; they spent eleven hours on set at Brockley Hall on August 23, and twelve hours the next day. They were ready for a break.

On Friday, August 23, Arthur called with their flight details. In a routine that had become familiar, Jane was to check with the airport about the exact arrival time in Augusta.

Arthur's last entry in his Day-Timer on August 25, 1985, lists their itinerary:

Gatwick BR# 221 11:30–14:10
JFK TW #903 4:15–5:21
BOS QO 1790 6:40–7:29

23

BAR HARBOR 1808

AUGUST 25, 1985, AUGUSTA, MAINE

Jane looked at the clock. It was past 9:30 p.m. Arthur and Sam's flight should be landing any moment now. This was Jane's second time to Augusta airport on Sunday, August 25. She had driven the five miles from her house in Manchester once before with one of Arthur's former students, Alan Blackwell, only to learn that Arthur and Sam's flight from Boston was delayed. This time she came alone, as Alan had to head home. The small terminal was virtually empty, save for the man at the airline counter and the taxi driver who worked out of the terminal.

Jane wondered what time they might wake up the next morning after such a long trip back home. Arthur told her their last two days in England had been especially long, and they were tired of hotel living. Sam was looking forward to spending time with her friends at the Maranacook Community School before their move to Los Angeles. Jane had been busy sorting through their belongings, trying to figure out what to take to California and what to sell at the garage sale. The last time Jane talked to Arthur, an exhausted Sam had been asleep in the hotel room.

She looked at the clock again. The scheduled arrival time had passed once again, but there was still no announcement. She was growing impatient. Then she looked over at the airline counter and saw the airline agent walk into the office and return to the counter looking very distressed. He eyed her momentarily and then disappeared back into the office. He emerged a moment later and walked over to her.

"I'm sorry, it's down." His voice was shaking.

"What does he mean?" Jane thought. Did they stop somewhere else? Was it a bumpy landing?

She looked at the man and asked, "What do you mean 'it's down'?"

The man stepped back. "The plane has crashed, ma'am."

Jane was surprised at her first thought: all alone in this, poor guy— she felt sorry for the man.

The plane was making an extra stop at Auburn-Lewiston and crashed on approach, the man said. When the meaning of his words finally sank in, Jane stood there stunned, unsure what to do next. She briefly considered driving to Auburn-Lewiston, some forty miles away. But she had no idea where the airport was in Auburn. She hoped Arthur and Sam had missed the flight. She walked over to the taxi stand and asked whether she could use the phone. She looked through her purse for their neighbor John Sexton's number. John knew the area well. Arthur would be happy to see John, she thought distractedly.

John was there in minutes. Jane hurried outside, forgetting her wallet on the counter.

It was taking forever to get to Auburn. "They are probably in the hospital by now," she thought. She then wondered what hospital they would be taken to.

At the Auburn-Lewiston airport, fire trucks and ambulances illuminated the night. Police were blocking off the road, not allowing anyone in. They got out of the car and walked up to the policeman. John said, "This is Jane Smith, Samantha Smith's mother. Her daughter and husband were on that plane." The policeman waved them through. Jane ran past the yellow tape toward the crash site. She tried to stay out of the responders' way, hoping that Arthur and Sam were there and were alive.

When she stopped to look down the ravine, she realized she'd been weeping the whole time. In the ravine lay the remnants of the plane, covered in foam. Among the darkened trees, the plane looked like a pile of ashes. It had missed the runway by over half a mile. Sam and Arthur were gone.

She had last talked to Sam a few days before, when they called from London.

"Mom, guess what I got?" Sam asked. Jane thought that someone might have given Sam a gift, or maybe she'd purchased a cute souvenir.

"My period!" Sam announced.

Poor Arthur had to deal with this on his own. It was just two dads with their daughters in London—Barney and Maia, Arthur and Sam. Sam didn't want to talk to her dad about it; Arthur wasn't that crazy about the event himself. Jane wanted to hear this and all their other stories again, imagining Sam's chatter interrupting her father's measured tone.

Fog and drizzling rain had plagued the East Coast earlier that day, turning Boston Logan Airport into a scene of confusion. Runways were congested with planes behind schedule; travelers, forced to make last-minute changes to their destinations, were frustrated. Arthur and Samantha's TWA flight from New York was supposed to arrive at 5:20 p.m. in Boston—in time for their Bar Harbor Flight 1790 to Augusta at 6:40 p.m. It's unclear whether they missed their original flight to Augusta or it was cancelled—as were many others that day—but later in the evening they were added to Bar Harbor Flight 1808, which was scheduled to arrive in Augusta at 9:40 p.m. Initially there were only four passengers, but then Bar Harbor added two more who were headed to Auburn-Lewiston, necessitating a stop there.

It would later emerge that one of the stranded passengers that night, a man named Steve Averill of Bangor, was about to take Bar Harbor 1808 after Delta announced yet another delay to his flight. Averill walked halfway to the Bar Harbor counter before reconsidering the "idea of flying in one of those fifteen-seaters and making all those stops." He turned around.

After some delay, at 9:17 p.m., Bar Harbor 1808 captain Roy Fraunhoffer notified Boston Clearance Delivery of their route to Auburn-Lewiston.

"I show you going to Augusta, is that correct?" the controller attempted to clarify.

"It's totally changed, first, ah, we'll take [the original flight plan] to Augusta and change it en route," replied Fraunhoffer.

With that, the controller cleared the plane for Augusta. They took off at 9:30 p.m. in what seemed like a routine departure.

About a half an hour later, at 9:58 p.m., Portland Approach cleared Flight 1808 for a Runway 4 approach at Auburn-Lewiston airport, which showed fog and light rain that night. Three minutes later, the plane appeared east of the course, and the controller inquired whether they were receiving the Lewiston localizer, the airport's system that assists in aligning with the runway.

"Not yet, we haven't intercepted."

The controller instructed them to turn left heading 340, which Fraunhoffer acknowledged.

Forty-five seconds later, the controller checked in again. "You're over Lewie. Now you receiving it?"

"Affirmative," answered Fraunhoffer.

The controller signed off. The pilot was told to contact the airport for any advisories or if he was unable to land on the first attempt. Once on the ground, he was to report on radio frequency 124.05.

The first officer acknowledged the instructions. This was the last transmission from Flight 1808.

With no black boxes aboard nonjet airplanes in 1985, high levels of noise in the Beechcraft 99 cockpit, and rain flowing down the plane's windshield, no one knows exactly what transpired on Flight 1808 in the last minutes of its approach to Auburn-Lewiston. The plane was off course and descending too fast over the unlit terrain. Declaring a missed approach—going around and trying to land again—would have been the preferred tactic, but Captain Fraunhoffer attempted to "salvage" the approach. For the next two minutes, he continued with what would later be referred to as an "unstabilized approach," unaware that he was flying too low. At about 10:05 p.m., the aircraft struck trees on Christian Hill, some four thousand feet short of the runway. It continued for over seven hundred feet before hitting the ground nearly upside down and then traveling along the grassy terrain for about 188 feet and coming to a halt in the ravine.

The flight path lay over Gerald and Florence Berwick's picnic table and the maple tree in front of their house in Auburn, but that night the plane clipped the stand of poplars nearby, one of the engines sounding like it had gone out and the other going "into a whine real fast." Florence couldn't get from one side of the house to the other before she heard the plane hit the ground in the woods behind the home of Renette and Stanley Gallagher. Inside, Gallagher, sure the plane would hit his home, dropped to his knees.

Days later, Joel Ryan, an investigator with the National Transportation Safety Board, would point to the poplars with the sheared-off tops, saying, "We know what happened in there." Then pointing at the blue stretch of sky behind him, he added, "We don't know what happened back there."

In the wreckage they found the *Lime Street* script, its pages untouched by the fire. A gold bracelet, a gift from Robert Wagner, inscribed with the filming date of *Lime Street*'s first episode, and a fancy paper bag with colored pads of note paper Samantha had picked up at one of the souvenir shops in London were also unharmed. Printed across the top of one pad was "So much work, so little time." Another proclaimed, "A peacock that sits on its tail feathers is just another turkey."

24

"A GREAT AMBASSADOR"

AUGUST 26, 1985, USSR / AUGUST 28, 1985, AUGUSTA, MAINE

On the evening of August 26, 1985, I was packing my schoolbag, wondering what the fourth grade would be like. Every school year in the Soviet Union started on the same day—September 1, my birthday. This one would be my tenth. I largely ignored the cacophony of the evening news broadcast on our black-and-white TV until it was suddenly interrupted by the commentator's somber voice: "The terrible news has just crossed the ocean. Samantha Smith is no more." I turned to the TV and froze.

In Fairfield, Connecticut, Helen D'Avanzo heard the news early in the morning and turned off the radio in her daughter Lynn's bedroom. When Lynn came out of her room and saw Helen's face, she thought that her grandma had passed away. "No," Helen said, "it's Sam." Lynn was in denial at first, hoping against hope that all of this was pretend, that everyone was doing this to protect Sam from the media. It simply couldn't be true.

At Maine's Alford Lake Camp, Jean McMullan, who had been instrumental in easing Sam's apprehension about camps just two short years earlier, heard the news on TV. Years later, she'd compare hearing about the crash that killed Samantha and Arthur to hearing the news of President John F. Kennedy's death: "I had the same terrible clutch at the stomach." Jean fell to her knees and wept.

In Switzerland, *Lime Street*'s director, Ray Austin, had just touched down at Gstaad International Airport when he got a call from Los Angeles. "Terrible news. Watch Robert Wagner because they are going to mob him with it. Samantha has been killed."

"What do you mean?" asked Austin.

"Well, Sam and her father completed most of their trip home. They were on the last leg of the journey when their plane crashed."

Austin knew that Wagner was on his way to the airport, so he asked his friends at Heathrow to watch for RJ and tell him to call Austin before he talked to anyone else.

On hearing the news of Samantha's death, Wagner was inconsolable.

"It was like my breath had left me," he would later write in his memoir. One of the show's writers, E. Jack Kaplan, later remembered Wagner saying, "Everyone around me dies."

In Leningrad, Natasha Kashirina couldn't believe the news of the crash at first. Then came the realization: "I will never see her again." She wished she'd written more to Samantha just as her mother had been telling her. "We have all the time in the world," Natasha would answer then. Now it was too late.

In Camp Artek, Olga and other counselors watched the news of the crash in disbelief. All over the Soviet Union, children and adults were stunned. "Samantha Smith will not be coming to us again," said a TV commentator. "They called her the young envoy of peace in the United States. And in the Soviet Union, she left behind thousands and thousands of friends." The Soviet youth newspaper, *Komsomoslkaya Pravda*, called her "a small person with a bold heart" and devoted more space to the story than to the death of high-ranking Soviet officials.

Jane didn't sleep much that first night. In the early morning hours, she felt an incredible rush of energy. She didn't know whether it was the fight-or-flight response, but at 5:00 a.m. she dressed and drove to the gym, hoping that it would be empty and that she'd be able to get rid of the inexplicable feeling before anyone had gotten a chance to hear the news. The thought that she'd have to live this tragedy out publicly filled her with dread.

The radio came on just as she started on the treadmill. She got off, picked up her clothes, and ran out of the gym. "People must have thought I was nuts," she said later, but in that moment she didn't know how else to cope.

Later that day the press was at her door. She mustered up the strength to come outside and read a statement that her friends Judy Bielecki and Ted Warner helped her put together:

> *Each generation contributes a building block for the next generation. As individuals, we are particles of earth from which the blocks are formed. I hope Samantha and Arthur have helped us realize how important each one of us can be.*
>
> *Samantha couldn't accept man's inhumanity to man. She stood fast in the belief that peace can be achieved and maintained by mankind. With her father supporting her actions, Samantha has contributed to the understanding among youth for conservation of our world.*

Soon the crash was all over the news, on TV and in the papers. "Samantha Smith dies in plane crash at 13," was a headline in the *Washington Post* on August 27, 1985. "Andropov's U.S. pen pal dies in crash," read the *Chicago Tribune*. Local papers and news stories ran pictures of smiling Sam on the set of *Lime Street* or holding up Andropov's reply alongside those taken at the crash site: mangled bits of metal strewn around a wooded path.

On August 27, a Western Union telegram arrived at Worthing Road in Manchester. Addressed to Mrs. Arthur Smith, it was sent from President and Mrs. Ronald Reagan's Santa Barbara home:

> *Nancy and I are profoundly saddened at the news of your great loss. A beloved husband and only daughter gone with shocking suddenness. I know that mere words can do little to ease the terrible pain of bereavement you must feel at this time. But perhaps you can take some measure of comfort from the knowledge that millions of Americans—indeed, millions of people throughout the world—share the burden of your grief. They too will always remember and cherish*

Samantha—her smile, her idealism, her unaffected sweetness of spirit. Nancy joins me in sending you our deepest sympathy. May God bless and console you. Ronald Reagan.

On August 28, 1985, people, some of them Arthur's former students, began arriving as early as 10:30 a.m. for a 1:00 p.m. service at St. Mary's Church in Augusta. "A small army of television and newspaper photographers . . . had set up camp in the shade of the maple trees" by the church entrance. Soon all the eight hundred seats were taken; only standing room remained. Another two hundred or so people crowded around the TV monitor set up outside. Still others watched from the post office steps and restaurant parking lot across Western Avenue.

"Not all spectators lining Western Avenue were there to mourn Samantha and her father Arthur," reported the papers. "Some just wanted a look at their first real live Russian, the enemy that Samantha had dared to say might have the same human hopes and fears that Americans have."

When a black limousine pulled up to St. Mary's doors, a tall man in his thirties stepped out. "The real live Russian" wore a tailored blue suit and had slicked-back hair. He looked surprisingly Western. Reporters closed ranks around him on the church steps. The man's name was Vladimir Kulagin, and he was the first secretary for cultural affairs at the Soviet embassy in Washington, DC. Kulagin had obtained a special clearance from the State Department to travel to Kennebec County, one of the ten Maine counties that were off limits to Soviet citizens in the summer of 1985. This concession was a rare pause in the Soviet-American conflict.

Kulagin paused and turned to the microphones. "She was like a ray of sunshine with her smile, her frankness, openness, her friendship. . . . We saw her, this small girl, as a big, great ambassador. You know? And . . . millions of Soviet people judged the American people by her." "And I believe," he continued, "the best monument to her will be that our peoples, our kids will go on with what she was doing—reaching to each other."

A few minutes later, another car pulled up to the curb. Jane, escorted by Robert Wagner, her brother Hank, and police officers, walked toward the church. She wore a white suit that day because she wanted the service to be a celebration of Sam's and Arthur's lives, not a mourning of their deaths.

Inside, the United Nations flag draped the podium; pots with red geraniums marked the ends of pews. A pair of white doves decorated a wreath of white chrysanthemums and red carnations bound by a white ribbon with "From the Embassy of the USSR" in gold lettering. One was from the elementary school in Hodgdon that Sam had attended when the Smiths lived in Amity. At the right of the altar was a wreath from Wagner, with a note: "In memory of Samantha who always was and always will be a joy to me." Another wreath was from Wagner's three daughters: Kate, Natasha, and Courtney.

Before the service began, Jane's brother Hank noticed a mic taped to a pew where he and Jane sat. Some reporter had hoped to record Jane's private conversations. Hank pulled it off and stepped on it.

"What gathers us here didn't begin with a tragic plane crash," said Reverend Peter Misner, a Methodist minister and the Smiths' neighbor. "What gathers us is a courageous child's question: 'Why are people afraid of each other? Why do people fight?'"

Sam's classmates as well as dignitaries spoke at the service. Sam's friend Dori Desautel described Sam as having "her mother's pretty face and her father's sense of humor." Maine governor Joseph E. Brennan spoke as well, calling Samantha "a very young girl who provided inspiration and hope not just for the very young, like herself, but for all of us. . . . The innocence of her youth, the sincerity of her beliefs, the magic of her smile melted the barriers between nations and warmed the hearts of the coldest diplomats. . . . No tragedy in recent memory has touched the hearts of so many," said Brennan. "At the corner store in Manchester, on Main Street, across our land, indeed in homes around the world there is deep sorrow."

William Prebble, Sam's adviser at Maranacook Community School in Readfield, said, "This little girl did things that governments don't have the power or the will to do. . . . Somehow, she managed to capture our collective fear of war." Prebble led a group of Sam's classmates in making a list of things they wanted to do before they died.

"We decided we'd like to travel, and we'd like to meet many people. We would want to make some contribution, and if we were successful at that, we wouldn't want to be stuck up or conceited. We agreed that Samantha had accomplished many of those things. . . . She had what most of us consider a full life. She never got stuck up or conceited. She always remained . . . giggly."

When Secretary Kulagin stepped up to the podium, he read a telegram from the new Soviet leader, Mikhail Gorbachev: "Please, accept my deepest condolences on the tragic death of your daughter Samantha and your husband Arthur. Everyone in the Soviet Union who knew Samantha Smith will remember forever the image of the American girl who, like millions of young Soviet men and women, dreamed about peace and about friendship between the peoples of the United States and the Soviet Union."

"Samantha shone like a brilliant beam of sunshine at a time when relations between our two countries were clouded," closed Kulagin.

Jane wanted to make sure that Arthur didn't "get lost in a shuffle" of people remembering Samantha, so she asked Rupert Neily, Arthur's good friend from their Ricker College days, to speak about him. "One of the things I liked most about Arthur . . . is that he would be unmerciful with me if I started to take myself too seriously . . . even on this occasion." He reflected on his friend and their time together at Ricker College. "Arthur was one of the finer examples of the soul and character of that remarkable little school. . . . He was a real and complete person to his students. . . . His wit and sense of humor were always at work and always at play. It seems that history has appointed this particular family to communicate an extraordinary message."

The children's choir sang "We Are the World," and the organist played "O God, Our Help in Ages Past" and "Let There Be Peace on Earth."

On September 8, Jane sent a thank-you card to the White House:

Dear Mr. President,

I'd like to thank you and Mrs. Reagan for your expression of sympathy on the loss of Arthur and Samantha.

In your telegram you mentioned that people will remember and cherish Samantha's idealism. Too often that term is equated with naivete, but in Samantha's case, her father and I felt that her dream of peaceful relations between the United States and the Soviet Union was based on the most practical of all considerations. She was able to see that whatever our differences and conflicting interests, when it comes to the need to avoid nuclear war, what is good for the Soviets is also good for us. That was why she was asking our leaders to work hard and fast to find the means to this mutually beneficial end.

I wish you and Mr. Gorbachev success in your upcoming meeting. People always say that our children are our future, but in this case, I really believe it is you who hold our future in your hands. My thoughts and good wishes will be with you.
Sincerely,
Jane G. Smith

The *Lime Street* series debuted on September 21. The producers asked Jane whether she wanted the filmed episodes to be shown. Sam would have wanted that, she said. By all accounts, Sam played her part brilliantly.

Mikhail Gorbachev and Ronald Reagan met in Geneva in November of that year, almost three years after Samantha penned her letter to the Kremlin. The Soviet and American leaders walked toward each other, their hands outstretched, and began the dialogue that would end the Cold War.

25

SAME

1985–1994, UNITED STATES AND SOVIET UNION

When the school bus passed Jane's house on the first day of school, it was hard for her not to see Sam run out of the house to catch it. In October 1985, two months after Sam and Arthur's passing, she established the Samantha Smith Foundation, its main goal being to promote under-standing between the peoples of the United States and the Soviet Union. It started with hundreds of sympathy cards, some of them with money to help continue what Sam had started. At first, she tried to work on the foundation alongside her full-time job, but soon she found herself on the phone late into the night. She was able to take a leave of absence from her job to become the president of the Samantha Smith Foundation. Its projects kept her very busy, something she desperately needed in those first months. Later, she discovered that the opportunity to talk about Sam and Arthur was a way to stay connected with them every day and a path to healing.

"We think of the Soviets as a bunch of dour old men who stand atop of Lenin's tomb and watch missiles parade by," Jane once said in an interview. "Somehow, we just never thought of them as humans. But they are. Humanity is what we have in common with the Russians. And while it's true that we can't expect the Soviets to become like us, what we can do is all learn to understand each other better."

After their summit in Geneva in November 1985, President Ronald Reagan and General Secretary Mikhail Gorbachev issued a joint statement, agreeing on the need "to intensify dialogue at various levels," and signed the Agreement on Contacts and Exchanges in Scientific, Educational, and Cultural Fields. They decided to "meet again in the nearest future" and invited each other to visit their respective countries. The statement noted that the leaders of the two nations believed that "there should be greater understanding among our peoples and that to this end they will encourage greater travel and people-to-people contact."

Just before Christmas that same year, at the Auburn Mall, a few miles away from the crash site, Governor Joseph E. Brennan launched a drive for the People of Maine's Memorial to Samantha Smith, unveiling a small replica of a statue that would be dedicated to Sam. The prototype was completed by sculptor Glenn Hines, Jane and Arthur's friend, whose sons had been Sam's friends when the Smiths lived in Amity. Governor Brennan read a letter from Soviet ambassador Anatoly Dobrynin, who remembered Samantha as "a little ambassador of peace and friendship between the Soviet and American people." President Reagan also sent a telegram on the opening of the memorial fund-raiser:

To Governor Brennan and the People of Maine:
I am pleased to send greetings to all those gathered for "The People of Maine's Memorial to Samantha Smith" inaugural event in Auburn, Maine.
Samantha's tragic and untimely death was felt deeply by the people of Maine, by all Americans, and by all who yearn for peace throughout the world. She was a young lady with great sensitivity and talent and her efforts seemed to embody the hopes we all hold for greater international understanding.
Nancy joins me in sending best wishes. God bless you.
Ronald Reagan

The completed full-size bronze statue of Samantha was dedicated in December 1986 by the Maine State Library and Museum, across from the state capitol building. The gold-trimmed plaque mounted on a neighboring stone read:

In 1982, ten year old Samantha Smith wrote a letter to Yuri Andropov, the leader of the Soviet Union asking, "Why do you want to go to war with the United States?" Mr. Andropov's reply to that letter, his invitation for Samantha to visit, and her subsequent trip with her parents to the Soviet Union, began a personal dialogue between the peoples of the Soviet Union and the United States that many believe contributed to the thaw in the dangerous Cold War of the late 20th Century.

Samantha's untimely death at age 13 in an airplane accident was mourned by adults and children world wide. Maine is proud of her native daughter and we remember the message she taught us:

One child can play a powerful part in bringing peace to the world.

On the other side of the ocean, in the fall of 1985, I searched my apartment for the *Pionerskaya Pravda* clippings that Baba Valia had saved for me two years earlier. Rummaging through the books on our bookshelf, I couldn't locate all the newspapers. "How could I have been so careless?" I was disappointed in my younger self. Record keeping suddenly became important. To my mom and Baba Valia's great delight, I finally started filing my own pictures in albums when I got them from school or friends rather than depositing them around the house.

The Samantha Smith scrapbook became the biggest project of my childhood, and I was determined to collect as much as I could. I asked everyone I knew to look through their subscriptions and share their findings with me. Once, when I saw an article I hadn't seen before displayed on the newspaper board at the local sports store, I realized that I didn't know anyone who subscribed to the *Sovetsky Sport* newspaper. Not sure how else to procure a copy, I walked back home and returned with a notebook and pencil. I stood in front of the newspaper board, oblivious to the curious onlookers, and copied down the article in its entirety by hand.

By then I had switched schools, having left my sports class at Arkhangelsk School #21 after a skating accident in the summer of 1984. An A in English in School #21 had allowed me to transfer without an exam to School #6, another specialized English school in town. There I made friends with another transfer from School #21, also named Lena, whom I, too busy with skating, had never gotten a chance to meet in the hallways of my old school. Lena Belogubova, a jovial blonde, a favorite of both girls and boys in School #6, quickly became my best friend. With figure skating out of the picture, I had a lot more free time too, and the two of us would ride to the Dvina River on Lena's bike, with me sitting on her handlebars, or bury time capsules under a tree near her apartment. Lena also became a faithful supporter of my quirky obsession with Samantha Smith, searching through her own family subscriptions for articles and sometimes walking the half hour to my apartment to deliver them.

Of course, my mom, worried that the sudden windfall of free time would be too much for me, started looking for other extracurriculars for me to get involved in. We briefly considered art school, but I didn't have enough drawings for the mandatory entry portfolio. The ones I did have, I feared, weren't good enough.

"Photography?" I suggested one summer evening at my mom's office because I thought it would be cool to capture light as it fell on the pot of violets on her windowsill. Since my mom's friend was a photography teacher at the Pioneer Palace, the decision was an easy one. Another opportunity presented itself one summer afternoon at the beach where we met a local chess school director who was looking for new students for his school. While I had never pictured myself as an Anatoly Karpov or Nonna Gaprindashvilli, the famous Soviet chess players, I found the director's explanations of chess moves intriguing enough, so I signed up.

The photography classes started that fall, and I soon learned how to open a film cassette in complete darkness and carefully put the film on a reel to develop, rinse, and set it. I fiddled with the photo enlarger to crop and enlarge images and hang them to dry in a red-tinted photography darkroom at the Pioneer Palace.

I found chess tedious—not nearly as exciting as photography. I discovered that I just couldn't sit still for long periods, and the chess theory teacher's monotonous narration of famous games as he moved chess figures with a ruler across a gigantic magnetic board bored me to tears. Yet the three years I spent at the chess school had their perks: they contributed to my steady good grades in math in middle school and earned me a few certificates of recognition at summer camps. But best of all, the chess school had an extensive newspaper collection, kept in boxes in a storage room next to the reception area. One day, bored with yet another chess theory class but not yet ready to head home, I asked the receptionist whether I could look through their subscriptions.

"Sure!" she said, confused as to why someone would want to look through old newspapers.

"Can I cut things out if I find what I'm looking for?" I was unrelenting.

"I suppose so," she said, clearly looking for me to stop asking.

Going to chess school suddenly was a lot more fun, and I would spend an hour or so every evening going through the old editions of Soviet newspapers. Soon my Samantha Smith scrapbook was filling out nicely.

The photography classes at the Pioneer Palace also proved useful in that regard. There I came across an issue of the *Sovetskoye Foto* magazine with a short "tips" article in which *Pionerskaya Pravda* photographer Vladimir Mashatin wrote about capturing Samantha Smith in Camp Artek. Mashatin wrote about the need to get creative in the pre-Photoshop days with the shots of Samantha and the crab. As I read the article, I realized that he was the same Vladimir Mashatin who had taken the picture of Samantha with the Russian doll that Baba Valia liked so much. I asked my photography teacher whether I could keep the article.

"Sure," he responded, since he was my mom's friend.

Three decades later, when I met Vladimir Mashatin in California, I told him that I had read about him in that *Sovetskoye Foto* magazine. He sent me a high-resolution black-and-white slide of the crab shot, along with many others of Samantha in Camp Artek, agreed to an interview, and organized an exhibit of his photographs of Samantha at the Maine State Library and Museum.

In the summer of 1986, Jane traveled to the Soviet Union, taking twenty-two of Samantha's classmates from Maranacook Community School to Moscow's Goodwill Games and to Camp Artek as part of the Soviet-American Memorial Exchange (or SAME) project, organized by Sam's advisor Bill Prebble, thus starting the unprecedented Soviet-American student exchanges of the 1980s. I learned about their trip in the article I copied down at the local sports store.

In September of that year, the National Transportation Safety Board (NTSB) completed its investigation into the crash of Flight 1808. They cited the captain's insistence on an unfeasible approach to landing as the probable cause. The NTSB also concluded that the air traffic controller had provided the crew with a radar vector that would cause the plane to come in at too great of an angle. Four pages of recommendations to increase aircraft safety in similar situations followed.

In August 1987, at the Alford Lake Camp in Hope, Maine, the preparations were being made for the first delegation of Soviet campers. Only four years earlier, in the summer of 1983, Alford Lake Camp director Jean McMullan had helped calm Sam's concerns about camps. Now president of the American Camp Association, Jean welcomed ten Soviet children and their four chaperones from Leningrad to Alford Lake Camp, where they were to spend a week alongside some of Samantha's classmates. They were the youngest cultural exchange group and the first to attend a US summer camp. At Samantha's statue, fifteen-year-old Tatyana Nikitina, who had met Samantha in Camp Artek, commented, "When I look at the monument of Samantha, and when I see so many people smiling with open faces and open hearts, I remember meeting Samantha."

One of the chaperones, Zinaida Dragunkina, echoed her comment: "We feel the warmness of the people who've been greeting us here. . . . We've been meeting so many nice, good people."

In 1986, in Arkhangelsk, I watched the first joint US/Soviet TV production, *Minneapolis-Moscow: A Children's Space Bridge*. Created in collaboration between Gosteleradio, the Soviet state TV, and WCCO in Minneapolis and hosted by American singer John Denver and Soviet journalist Vladimir Pozner, it was "dedicated to the spirit of Samantha Smith." In the pre-Internet days, the "space bridge" was unique, as it allowed Soviet and American children to see each other in real time, reach out across the ocean, and sing together in a play called *Peace Child*. What had seemed impossible just a few short years earlier was happening right in front of my eyes. "My generation will be different," I thought; we could make this world a better place.

In June 1988, Jane traveled to the Soviet Union as part of "a small American contingent invited to Moscow" during the summit between Ronald Reagan and Mikhail Gorbachev. Together with Valentina Tereshkova and Natalia Batova, Jane was among the guests at the Bolshoi Theater ballet performance hosted in honor of the summit. When the Reagans and Gorbachevs arrived at the theater, the audience greeted them with thunderous applause. As Jane listened to the American anthem, followed by the Soviet anthem, and watched the two leaders stand next to each other, she wondered what Sam might have thought about these developments. This had been nearly unthinkable just a few years earlier. Yet there they were, and Jane could see them with her own eyes. Sam, she was sure, would have thought all of this simply terrific.

The Soviets honored Samantha by issuing a commemorative stamp and naming a diamond, a mountain, a cultivar of tulips, and an asteroid after her. In Maine, Governor John McKernan signed a bill proclaiming the first Monday in June as Samantha Smith Day.

The Samantha Smith Foundation continued to organize Soviet-American exchanges, working with many camps in Maine, New Hampshire, Connecticut, New York, and Vermont, as well as with several camps in the Soviet Union. Jean McMullan remained a steady supporter of the efforts. In Poland, Maine, Jay and Karen Stager dedicated their two-hundred-acre camp to Samantha, naming it the Samantha Smith World Peace Camp, and, in collaboration with the Samantha Smith Foundation, hosted hundreds of Soviet young people there in the early 1990s. Samantha's Artek friend Natasha Kashirina and her counselor Olga were Samantha Smith World Peace Camp counselors in the summer of 1990.

In June of the same year, the foundation arranged for a Soviet military plane to transport seventy-seven children and twenty adults from the region of Bryansk near Chernobyl, the site of the 1986 nuclear disaster, to Pease Air Force base in New Hampshire. As the caravan from the Samantha Smith World Peace Camp was waved through security at Pease, they watched the Soviet plane land and taxi past Air Force One. As the Soviet Union began to explore the idea of a free market system, the Samantha Smith Foundation pioneered placement of young business interns in Maine businesses with its Job Shadow Program.

By 1991, the Soviet Union had fallen apart. The Cold War was over. Jane continued her work as president of the Samantha Smith Foundation into the early 1990s, but the relations between the two countries were normalizing, and soon the foundation fell victim to its own success. Travel between the United States and the Soviet Union had opened up, and other exchanges had sprung up in schools and universities. The idea that the people of the United States and the Soviet Union used to see each other as enemies finally seemed a relic of the past.

Now, almost forty years later, nuclear war seems like a possibility once again. Samantha's innocent curiosity about the other side of the Iron Curtain during a tumultuous time in history serves as a reminder to never stop questioning the status quo and to recognize that the preservation of peace is not only the responsibility of governments. She taught us all a mighty lesson: every one of us, every ordinary child and adult, has the power to change the world.

EPILOGUE

JULY 2021, MAINE

"Look at the license plate." My husband pointed out a car in a parking lot in Portland, Maine, in the summer of 2021. On it was a picture of a father and daughter, hand in hand, walking away into the sunset. The image on the vanity plate in support of Maine agriculture seemed serendipitous—I was almost done writing Samantha Smith's story.

On a warm and humid afternoon that July, I drove past the Smiths' old house on Worthing Road in Manchester. Not wanting to disturb its current occupants, I parked on the side of the road past the house and stepped out to look around. The warm air smelled of wild rose—just like Arkhangelsk in summer. By the roadside, the tall green thickets seemed to have transplanted themselves from behind the *dereviashka* in my childhood yard by the Sleeping Skyscraper. Somewhere in these woods, Sam and Lynn had looked for the end of the stream, I thought. In the summer of 1983, back in Arkhangelsk, I had surveyed the world from my perch atop the motorcycle tree—around me the same kind of green, the same summer air. How similar our childhoods were in the Russian North and US Northeast, and yet how different.

I looked through the trees and tried to imagine the loud chatter on the front steps of the Smiths' home back in July 1983—Arthur and Jane, Sam, Nonnie, and friends taking pictures before heading to the airport. I looked at the white clapboard houses along the small country road that they left behind that summer to travel to the vastly unknown Soviet Union, never to return to their pre-"Sam's adventure" normal. I stood there for a while thinking of what might have been if they had stayed home.

If you take a trip to Amity, Maine, as my husband and I did that July, you might not see a single car for miles on end. A small town of 253 people (as per the 2020 census) in the densely wooded area of Aroostook County near the Canada-US border, Amity is very remote. Even fewer people lived there in 1972 when Sam was born. The field next to the Smiths' old house on Lycette Road, where Sam liked to play with her dog Gar, is now a small forest. At the farmers' market on Main Street in neighboring Houlton, we bought a blueberry pie and strolled up and down the streets of what used to be Ricker College. I imagined little Sam with pigtails, holding Arthur's hand as the two of them walked to his English class.

My journey from Arkhangelsk to Amity was a remarkably long one—I started at the age of seven with seeing Samantha, my first American, on my black-and-white TV and then collecting newspaper articles about her journey in my country. It took me almost forty years to arrive where Samantha's journey began—in her hometown on the other side of the ocean. Only in Amity did I truly understand what Jane had always said: "Samantha was just an ordinary girl." Samantha Smith was indeed an ordinary girl from a very ordinary town. She didn't like moving or camps, and yet she traveled to the distant Soviet Union to meet people everyone considered enemies. And with that, this seemingly ordinary girl rose to an extraordinary challenge and became a young ambassador with a message of hope for the world.

That summer, I also stood near the fence on Foster Road, from which point I could watch planes land on Runway 4 at Auburn-Lewiston airport. A light afternoon breeze shuffled the leaves in the woods nearby. Two small airplanes flew overhead, clearing the trees at just the right altitude and landing safely on the runway. One and then another.

There are so many what-ifs in the story of Samantha Smith. What if Jane and Arthur had never left Amity? What if Samantha had never written her letter or come to the phone at Manchester Elementary in April 1983? What if she had decided not to go to the Soviet Union? What if, on her return, Arthur and Jane had never let her do television? What if she had lived?

Jane, who was left behind to carry on, was once asked whether she would do it again. "I've thought about it," she said, "but I'd do the same thing again. It was good for Samantha, and it was good for the world. We had a lot of fun as a family during that time. The only thing I would have asked was that it had lasted longer."

I graduated from School #6 in the spring of 1992 and was accepted into the Foreign Languages Department at the Pomor State University in Arkhangelsk—my dream was to become a teacher of English. That summer I also got a job as an interpreter with an American humanitarian organization. By the end of that summer, I found the job both fun and educational, so I left my university studies and continued in humanitarian work for the next fifteen years. That is where I met my husband, an American. Baba Valia liked him right away. I moved to California in 1995 but traveled to Russia frequently and witnessed many of the changes in my country. My work took me to many fascinating places around the world. Eventually, I did become a teacher of English, having completed both undergraduate and graduate studies in the United States. My husband and I have two children, a boy and a girl, who grew up with a Russian *baba* and an American grandma.

"You're the happy ending to Sam's story," Jane told me not so long ago.

I don't quite agree. I think that my entire generation of Soviet and American children of the 1980s are the happy ending to the story of Samantha Smith. The little girl from a tiny town in Maine showed us that peace was possible if we just made an effort to reach out and get to know each other. Because of that simple message, we survived the Cold War.

ACKNOWLEDGMENTS

When I was unsure whether I'd be able to do something on my own as a child, my grandmother Baba Valia would often say, "This world isn't without kind people," to remind me not to give up. Help would come, she knew from experience, from kind people along the way. I clung to her saying when I started on the journey of writing this book, because when Jane, Samantha's mother, first suggested that I do so, I had no idea how one would go about writing and publishing a book. And so it was through the kindness of others that this book came into being.

First and foremost, my eternal gratitude goes to Jane: thank you for sharing your family's story, for connecting me with many of the sources, for opening your home and your archive, and for your unending kindness and patience with my many questions. Thank you for Samantha and for believing that I could tell her story.

When I first began working on this book in the summer of 2015, my professors and classmates in the UCLA Writers' Program became my very first readers. Gordon Grice encouraged my first attempts, and Dr. Yelizaveta Renfro suggested the braided narrative that helped me make sense of the structure. When I was lost on the topic of book proposals, I signed up for a class with Kristen Loberg, and her generosity, kindness, and expert advice kept me going when the going was tough. Thank you to my classmates at the UCLA Writers' Program who read the first drafts of these chapters, especially Dr. Nancy Pine, Dr. Kimber Del Valle, and Marlene McCurtis.

As I continued working on the book, I drew my strength from my writing group—initially at the Vroman's Bookstore in Pasadena, led by Barbara Abercrombie, and then on its Zoom Covid Campus, led by

Lauren Tyler-Rickon. For two years (and counting), Lauren became the voice that inspired us to keep writing. To Marilyn Davis, Dr. James Garbanati, Dr. Alexandra Levine, Michelle Peterson, Dr. Jean Richardson, Valerie Silverio, Nora Sun, and Anne Witzgall: my eternal gratitude for your undying support, kindness, and invaluable insights into the early drafts of this manuscript (as well as putting up with my reading something almost every meeting). Thank you for being my deadlines and hence my lifelines as this book came into existence. I couldn't have done this without you.

A special thank-you to Michael Steere, my editor at Down East Books, for taking a chance on me and shepherding this book to publication! I am also grateful for the assistance provided by copyeditor Jen Kelland.

I want to thank people who knew Samantha and were willing to help me tell her story: Natalia Batova, Helen D'Avanzo, Lynn D'Avanzo, John Dougherty, Hank Goshorn, Glenn and Diane Hines, Felicia Kornbluh, Anne Lambert, Vladimir Mashatin, Jean McMullan, Jean O'Niell, Barbara Quill, Natalia Rosston, Thomas Simons, Tara Sonenshine, Olga Volkova, Robert Wagner, and Jack Weible. Special thanks to Valery Kostin, who shared a lot about the history of Camp Artek and helped me connect with one of its favorite counselors, and to Arnold Shapiro, who was instrumental in helping with the Disney chapter and whose work ethic is truly inspirational.

When it came to researching this book, I'm very grateful to Jennifer Mandel at the Ronald Reagan Presidential Library & Museum for her patience with the onslaught of my email inquiries, and to Laurie LaBar, Natalie Liberace, Benjamin Stickney, and Sarah Stanton at the Maine State Museum in Augusta for their help with locating the materials from the Samantha Smith Collection. Thank you also to the Temecula Public Library staff in Temecula, California, for their assistance with the interlibrary loans and setting up the microfilm machine for me—I was only the second person to use it that year! Thank you to the staff at the Russian State Archive of Contemporary History for their assistance in locating the Russian-language documents about Samantha. I'm thankful to Dr. Anton Fedyashin at the American University in Washington, DC, for sharing his research into Samantha's story. And, of course, to my dear friend Lena Belogubova for helping my Samantha Smith collection grow with her family's subscriptions when we were kids.

I also want to thank some of the early supporters of www.Saman thaSmith.info, the website I made in Samantha's memory, especially Sergei Sorokin for the very first contributions to its archive; Yulia Baryshnikova for scanning her Samantha Smith collection and locating the *Pravda* article at her local library; and Emir Mendoza for his help in setting up the original website gallery and maintaining it for close to a decade. A big thank-you also to many others who over the years have sent me their collections of Samantha articles and pictures and supported the website in other ways, among them Ekaterina Dobrynina, Steven Guinn, David Hagen, Victor Matrosov, Robert A. Medeiros, Tracy Lynn Meyers, and Irina Pavlova. Thank you also to the late Millard L. Gower, whose meticulous record of local articles on the crash made its way to me and was of great help in writing the "Bar Harbor 1808" chapter.

There were times when the project seemed too overwhelming, and then help would come—by the way of encouragement from friends and strangers. To my best friend, Ingrid Støle: thank you for always being there, having faith in me, and celebrating victories big and small. To Geoff Johns and Jamie Iracleanos: thank you for believing in this story!

When it was time to find a publisher, I relied on the treasure trove of information that is Jane Friedman—big hearts like yours lift a lone artist's spirits. Thank you for your insights on my proposal, your book *The Business of Being a Writer*, and your website www.JaneFriedman.com, a wonderful resource for an aspiring author! When I found the publisher but had no idea how to negotiate the publishing contract, Rosanna Xia came to the rescue—thank you for your time and willingness to help a fellow writer.

My gratitude also goes to writers I've never met. Rebecca Skloot—I found so much hope in your quest for Henrietta Lacks' story. Thank you for saying, "That core of obsession is the first and most important criteria for writing any story." I suspected I had the obsession, but your relentless pursuit of your story inspired me to keep going with Samantha's. I'm also grateful to Jackson Bliss, whose posts about "good rejections" (yes, there are those!) sustained me through many of my own, good and bad (http://www.jacksonbliss.com).

Of course, I will always be grateful to Baba Valia for introducing me to Samantha's story and to my mom, who supported my childhood preoccupation by helping me find articles and buying me the Russian version of the *Journey to the Soviet Union* and the Samantha Smith postage stamp when it came out in the Soviet Union.

A big thank-you goes to my family. To my husband, Ken, who read the many revisions of the same chapters: thank you for your patience and for spotting the missing "the" or "a"—because tired Russians are prone to missing articles nonexistent in their native tongue, even if they have a graduate degree in linguistics and teach English as a second language. To my children, Kenny and Nikki, who, along with their dad, accompanied me on several of my pilgrimages to Maine and were very good-natured about having to wait as I looked through stacks of articles and took pictures or notes. A special thank-you to Nikki, a future English teacher, for reading many of these chapters and providing vital perspective.

Finally, thank you to all the schoolchildren (and their parents) who have written to me over the years wanting to know more about Samantha. Thank you for keeping her memory alive! One person can make a difference!

REFERENCES

ABCNews.com. "Samantha Smith Getting Ready for the Trip to the USSR [1983]." Video posted to YouTube by SamanthaSmithINFO. https://www.youtube.com/watch?v=MHPnmaC4sEE (accessed November 22, 2021).

Allen, Mel. "Life after Samantha." *Yankee Classic.* May 1988.

Bellamy, Earl, and Ray Austin, dirs. *Lime Street.* Culver City, CA: Sony Pictures Television, 1985.

Blake, Patricia. "A Top Cop Takes the Helm." *Time.* November 22, 1982.

Boxer, Tim. "TV." *New York Post.* October 19, 1984.

Bukvar. Букварь. Prosveshenie, 1982.

Burns, John F. "Brezhnev Dead at 75, No Successor Named; Reagan Pledges an Effort to Improve Ties." *New York Times.* November 12, 1982.

Central Intelligence Agency, Office of the Director of Central Intelligence. "Job 83M00914R: Executive Director and Executive Registry Files (1982), Box 20, Folder 3, L–205A McMahon Grams. Secret." Office of the Historian. November 19, 1982. https://history.state.gov/historicaldocuments/frus1981-88v03/d240 (accessed November 22, 2021).

Chernyaev, Anatoly. "Дневники А. С. Черняева [Diaries of A.S. Chernyaev]. 1982." National Security Archive. https://nsarchive.gwu.edu/rus/text_files/Chernyaev/1982.pdf (accessed November 4, 2021).

———. "Дневники А. С. Черняева [Diaries of A.S. Chernyaev]. 1983." National Security Archive. https://nsarchive.gwu.edu/rus/text_files/Chernyaev/1983.pdf (accessed January 10, 2022).

Citizen News Services. "Samantha Leaves for Moscow Date." *Ottawa Citizen.* July 8, 1983.

Datz, Bob. "Samantha." Unknown. 1983.

De Paul, Tony. "She Touched Many Hearts." *Bangor Daily News.* August 29, 1985.

Dobrynin, Anatoly. *In Confidence.* New York: Times Books, 1995.

"The Doomsday Clock." Bulletin of the Atomic Scientists. https://the bulletin.org/doomsday-clock/timeline (accessed November 22, 2021).

Downing, Taylor. *1983.* New York: DaCapo Press, Hachette Book Group, 2018.

Drischler, Alvin Paul. Letter to Mr. Matthew, September 8, 1983, ID #154386. WHORM: Subject File: PC, Topic Guide: Samantha Smith. Ronald Reagan Presidential Library & Museum. https:// www.reaganlibrary.gov/public/digitallibrary/whormsubject/co165/ 40-654-6235777-CO165-154386-2017.pdf (accessed July 5, 2020).

Druzhinin, Alexander. "Meet Samantha. Познакомьтесь с Самантой [1983]." Video posted to YouTube by SamanthaSmithINFO. https://www.youtube.com/watch?v=VFlcL8ebWPs&t=44s (accessed August 26, 2015).

"Eastern European Changes Mind-Boggling, Smith Says." *Sun Journal.* December 18, 1989.

"11-Year-Old Girl Leaves for Russia, Andropov's Guest." *Lakeland Ledger.* July 8, 1983.

Federal Archive Agency. "Состоится открытие историко— документальной выставки «Андропов. К 100-летию со дня рождения» [Federal Archive Agency—opening of the historical and documentary exhibition 'Andropov. 100th anniversary of birth' is planned]." Federal Archive Agency. September 6, 2014. http:// archives.gov.ru/index.php?q=exhibitions/2014-andropov_press .shtml (accessed July 10, 2015).

Fedyashin, Anton. "Andropov's Gamble: Samantha Smith and Soviet Soft Power." *Journal of Russian American Studies* 4, no. 1 (May 4, 2020): 1–23. https://journals.ku.edu/jras/article/view/13656 (accessed June 7, 2020).

Fischer, Ben B. "The Cold War Conundrum: The 1983 Soviet War Scare." CIA Freedom of Information Act Electronic Reading Room. September 1997. https://www.cia.gov/readingroom/docs/19970901.pdf.

Fleming, Jon. "Samantha Plans Visit to Russia with 'Secret Gift' for Andropov." UPI Archives. June 23, 1983. https://www.upi.com/Archives/1983/06/23/Samantha-plans-visit-to-Russia-with-secret-gift-for-Andropov/1671425188800 (accessed April 21, 2018).

Fredericks, Arthur. "Samantha Smith." *Bryan Times*. August 29, 1985.

Gale, Michael. Memorandum for Faith Ryan Whittlessey, "Samantha Smith and Avi Goldstein," July 11, 1983. Matlock, Jack F.: Files. Folder Title: USSR General [1981-1983] (5). Box 26. Ronald Reagan Presidential Library & Museum. https://www.reaganlibrary.gov/public/digitallibrary/smof/nsc-europeanandsovietaffairs/matlock/box-026/40-351-7452065-026-006-2018.pdf (accessed January 16, 2022).

Gillette, Robert. "Unlike American Child, Irina Fails to Move Yuri." *Los Angeles Times*. June 13, 1983.

"Girl Brings Present to Yuri Andropov." *Tuscaloosa News*. July 8, 1983.

Goldstein, Avi. Letter to Samantha Smith, May 10, 1983. Matlock, Jack F.: Files. Folder Title: USSR General [1981–1983] (5). Box 26. P. 5, 6. Ronald Reagan Presidential Library & Museum. https://www.reaganlibrary.gov/public/digitallibrary/smof/nsc-europeanandsovietaffairs/matlock/box-026/40-351-7452065-026-006-2018.pdf (accessed January 16, 2022).

Golz, Glenn. "Samantha Smith's Friends Prepare for Trip to Russia." *Bangor Daily News*. May 24, 1985.

"Gorbachev Sends Telegram to Samantha Smith's Mom." *Register-Guard*. August 28, 1985.

"Governor Praises Girl at Home Town Parade." *Sarasota Herald Tribune*. July 24, 1983.

Hale, John. "Kindling the Spirit of Friendship." Unknown. 1987.

Harriman, Averell. "Memorandum of Conversation between General Secretary Yuri Andropov and Averell Harriman Written by Harriman, 3:00 PM. June 2 1983, CPSU Central Committee

Headquarters, Moscow, Unclassified." National Security Archive. June 2, 1983. https://nsarchive.gwu.edu/document/17311-document-11-memorandum-conversation-between (accessed January 10, 2022).

Higgins, Anne. Suggested Reply to Donald Jelks, May 23, 1983, ID #142046. WHORM: Subject File: PC, Topic Guide: Samantha Smith. Ronald Reagan Presidential Library & Museum. https://www.reaganlibrary.gov/public/digitallibrary/whormsubject/pc/40-654-2825101-PC-142046-2017.pdf (accessed July 5, 2020).

"HD Soviet Leader Leonid Brezhnev Funeral." Video posted to YouTube by RedSamurai84, November 15, 1982. https://www.youtube.com/watch?v=1ZyDTIt3xE4 (accessed October 29, 2021).

"History of Artek." Artek. https://artek.org/ob-arteke/istoriya (accessed January 15, 2022).

Huntington, Tom. *Maine at 200: An Anecdotal History Celebrating Two Centuries of Statehood*. Lanham, MD: Down East Books, 2020.

"Информационное сообщение о пленуме Центрального Комитета Коммунистической Партии Советского Союза [Information Message about the Plenum of the Central Committee of the Communist Party of the Soviet Union]." *Sovetskaya Rossiya*. November 13, 1982.

ITN Source. "Samantha Smith Prepares for Her Trip to USSR—Archival Footage [1983]." Video posted to YouTube by Samantha SmithINFO. https://www.youtube.com/watch?v=XxN8N87mgMw (accessed January 10, 2022).

Jelks, Donald. Telegram to President Reagan, April 26, 1983, ID #142046. WHORM: Subject File: PC, Topic Guide: Samantha Smith. Ronald Reagan Presidential Library & Museum. https://www.reaganlibrary.gov/public/digitallibrary/whormsubject/pc/40-654-2825101-PC-142046-2017.pdf (accessed July 5, 2020).

"Joint Soviet-United States Statement on the Summit Meeting in Geneva." American Presidency Project. November 21, 1985. https://www.presidency.ucsb.edu/documents/joint-soviet-united-states-statement-the-summit-meeting-geneva (accessed September 5, 2021).

Kernan, Michael. "The Maine Land, Ready for Samantha." *Washington Post.* July 22, 1983.

Kliff, Barry. "The Littlest Diplomat Takes Peace Plea to Moscow." *Montreal Gazette.* July 8, 1983.

Kolmanovsky, Eduard. "Хотят ли русские войны [Do the Russians want war]." 1961.

Krasnova, T., I. Afanasiev, and V. Mashatin. "Я люблю тебя, Артек! [I love you, Artek!]." *Pionerskaya Pravda.* July 19, 1983.

Krauthammer, Charles. "Essay: Deep Down, We're All Alike, Right? Wrong." *Time.* August 15, 1983.

———. "Kids' Stuff." *New Republic.* February 13, 1984.

Krechetnikov, Artem. "Брежнев: как стабильность превратилась в застой." BBC.com. November 9, 2012. https://www.bbc.com/russian/russia/2012/11/121109_brezhnev_stability_stagnation (accessed March 30, 2021).

Lahammer, Gene. "Joint Minneapolis-Moscow TV Program Announced." *AP News.* October 24, 1985. https://apnews.com/article/d35b6c575bc0ce3b69c8d7f6144f99bf.

Lannin, Joanne. "Flight 1808: What Happened?" Unknown. 1985.

Lebedev-Kumach, Vasily. "Священная Война [Sacred war]." 1941.

Lenczowski, John. Memo for Robert M. Kimmitt, "Proposal to Invite Soviet Youth to U.S.," August 9, 1983. Matlock, Jack F.: Files. Folder Title: USSR General [1981–1983] (5). Box 26. P. 7. Ronald Reagan Presidential Library & Museum. https://www.reaganlibrary.gov/public/digitallibrary/smof/nsc-europeanandsovietaffairs/matlock/box-026/40-351-7452065-026-006-2018.pdf (accessed January 16, 2022).

"List of *The Tonight Show Starring Johnny Carson* episodes (1983)." Wikipedia. https://en.wikipedia.org/wiki/List_of_The_Tonight_Show_Starring_Johnny_Carson_episodes_(1983) (accessed November 18, 2021).

Marchek, Elizabeth A. "Hometown Fetes Samantha." *Bulletin.* July 24, 1983.

Mashatin, Vladimir. "Бантики для Саманты [Bows for Samantha]." *Novye Izvestiya.* July 12, 2013. https://newizv.ru/news/

society/12-07-2013/185501-bantiki-dlja-samanty (accessed January 15, 2022).

Matlock, Jack. Memo to William P. Clark, "New Map of Areas Closed to Soviet Diplomats," August 2, 1983. Matlock, Jack F.: Files. Folder Title: Diplomatic—USSR (3). Box 22. Ronald Reagan Presidential Library & Museum. https://www.reaganlibrary.gov/public/digitallibrary/smof/nsc-europeanandsovietaffairs/matlock/box-022/40-351-7452065-022-005-2018.pdf (accessed July 5, 2020).

———. Note. Matlock, Jack F.: Files. Folder Title: USSR General [1981–1983] (5). Box 26. P. 10. Ronald Reagan Presidential Library & Museum. https://www.reaganlibrary.gov/public/digitallibrary/smof/nsc-europeanandsovietaffairs/matlock/box-026/40-351-7452065-026-006-2018.pdf (accessed January 16, 2022).

Matthew, Morton P. Letter to Honorable Nancy L. Johnson, July 11, 1983, ID #154386. WHORM: Subject File: PC, Topic Guide: Samantha Smith. Ronald Reagan Presidential Library & Museum. https://www.reaganlibrary.gov/public/digitallibrary/whormsubject/co165/40-654-6235777-CO165-154386-2017.pdf (accessed July 5, 2020).

National Transportation Safety Board (NTSB). "Aircraft Accident Report: Bar Harbor Airlines Flight 1808, Beech B-99, N300WP, Auburn Lewiston Municipal Airport, Auburn, Maine, August 25, 1985." NTSB/AAR-86/06. NTSB. http://libraryonline.erau.edu/online-full-text/ntsb/aircraft-accident-reports/AAR86-06.pdf (accessed August 14, 2015).

"Negatives—1983 Soviet Trip." 2010.37.168.4. Collections of the Maine State Museum.

Oberdorfer, Don. *From the Cold War to a New Era: The United States and the Soviet Union, 1983–1991.* Baltimore: Johns Hopkins University Press, 1998.

"Parade Today for Samantha." *Gadsden Times.* July 24, 1983.

"Peer of Samantha Smith Says Her Story Inspired His Life Aspirations." News Center Maine. April 26, 2018. https://www.newscentermaine.com/article/features/samantha-smith/97-544557002.

REFERENCES

"President Reagan's Address to the Nation on the Soviet Attack on a Korean Airliner (KAL 007) on September 5, 1983." Video posted to YouTube by the Reagan Foundation on April 23, 2011. https://www.youtube.com/watch?v=9VA4W1wDMAk&t=90s (accessed January 17, 2022).

Quill, Barbara. *To Russia with Love*. WGAN, 1983.

Quinn, Francis X. "Samantha Welcomed by Parade." *Lewiston Daily Sun*. July 25, 1983.

Rawson, Davis. "More Than 1,000 Mourn Samantha." *Bangor Daily News*. August 29, 1985.

Reagan, Ronald. "Remarks at the Annual Convention of the National Association of Evangelicals in Orlando, Florida." Ronald Reagan Presidential Library & Museum. March 8, 1983. https://www.reaganlibrary.gov/archives/speech/remarks-annual-convention-national-association-evangelicals-orlando-fl.

———. Telegram to Mrs. Jane Smith, August 27, 1985. WHORM Subject File Code: ME001-03, Case file Number(s): 343256. Ronald Reagan Presidential Library & Museum. https://www.reaganlibrary.gov/public/digitallibrary/whormsubject/me001-03/40-654-12019891-ME001-03-343256-2017.pdf (accessed February 4, 2022).

Reed, Steven. "Samantha Smith Thought Her First Ballet Would Be Dull . . ." *UPI*. July 16, 1983. https://www.upi.com/Archives/1983/07/16/Samantha-Smith-thought-her-first-ballet-would-be-dull/9835427176000.

Romano, Lois. "Samantha Smith: On to Journalism." *Washington Post*. January 20, 1984.

Rosston, Natalia. "Natasha Kashirina Remembers." SamanthaSmith.info. August 2015. http://www.samanthasmith.info/index.php/2-uncategorised/140-natasha-kashirina-remembers (accessed January 15, 2022).

"Samantha and the Soviets Special [July 25, 1983]." Video posted to YouTube by SamanthaSmithINFO. https://www.youtube.com/watch?v=5OfFodDS1P0.

"Samantha Plans Soviet Visit, But . . ." *Bangor Daily News*. June 17, 1983.

"Samantha Praised by Governor." *Bangor Daily News*. July 25, 1983.

Samantha Smith Center. "The Children of Chernobyl Arrive!" *Samantha Smith Center Newsletter*. 1990.

———. "Greetings from Jane." *Samagram Newsletter*. Fall 1989.

———. "Our Major Business Program Expands." *Samantha Smith Center Newsletter*. Spring 1993.

"Samantha Smith Dies in Maine Plane Crash." *Orlando Sentinel*. August 26, 1985.

Samantha Smith Foundation. "Soviet Teens Arrive Next Week for the Samantha Smith Foundation Exchange." Press Release. Samantha Smith Foundation. 1986.

"Samantha Smith Has Role in TV Series with Robert Wagner." *Lewiston Daily Sun*. February 26, 1985.

"Samantha Smith Plans Letter to President Reagan." *Bangor Daily News*. May 11, 1983.

"Samantha Starts Trip to Russia." *Spokane Chronicle*. July 7, 1983.

"Samantha Tired, Happy after Soviet Union Trip." *Boca Raton News*. July 24, 1983.

"Samantha Tours Japanese Cities." *Spokane Chronicle*. December 21, 1983.

"Samantha: There Is No Place Like Home as Two Week Trip Ends." *Miami News*. July 23, 1983.

"Samantha's Visit." *Times News*. December 23, 1983.

Schnurmacher, Thomas. "Catya Sassoon: Hair Apparent Daughter on Her Own." *Montreal Gazette*. March 16, 1985.

Shapiro, Arnold, and Jean O'Neill. *Samantha Smith Goes to Washington: Campaign '84*. Burbank, CA: Disney Channel, 1984.

Shultz, George P. *Turmoil and Triumph*. New York: Macmillan, 1993.

Smith, Jane. Letter to Ronald Reagan, September 8, 1985. WHORM Subject File Code: ME001-03. Case file Number(s): 340137 Topic Guide: Samantha Smith. Ronald Reagan Presidential Library & Museum. https://www.reaganlibrary.gov/public/digital

library/whormsubject/me001-03/40-654-12019891-ME001-03
-340317-2017.pdf.

———. "The Spirit of Samantha." *Woman's World*. December, 1989.

Smith, Samantha. Interview by Johnny Carson. *The Tonight Show Starring Johnny Carson*. April 29, 1983.

———. Interview by Johnny Carson. *The Tonight Show Starring Johnny Carson*. July 28, 1983.

———. Interview by Ted Koppel. *Nightline*. April 25, 1983.

———. *Journey to the Soviet Union*. Boston: Little, Brown, 1985.

———. Letter to Yuri Andropov. Российский Государственный Архив Новейшей Истории (Russian State Archive of Contemporary History—RGANI) f. 82 (Andropov, Yuri Vladimirovich [1914–1984], General Secretary of CC CPSU, Chairman of the Presidium of the Supreme Soviet of the USSR), op. 1, d. 61, l. 8. 1982.

———. "Samantha Smith on The Today Show and The Phil Donahue Show [February 18, 1984]." Video posted to YouTube by Maine Public. https://www.youtube.com/watch?v=AoQ_Lji5V70.

Snauffer, Douglas. *The Show Must Go On: How the Deaths of Lead Actors Have Affected Television*. Jefferson, NC: McFarland, 2008.

"Soviet Envoy Attends Rites for Samantha." *Los Angeles Times*. August 28, 1985. https://www.latimes.com/archives/la-xpm-1985-08-28 -mn-24933-story.html.

Sullivan, Jennifer. "Blessed Are the Peacemakers: 1,000 Throng to Memorial Service for Arthur and Samantha Smith." *Sun*. August 1985.

"Sweet Samantha Brings Maple Syrup and Candy Canes on Her Tour of Japan." *Montreal Gazette*. December 23, 1983.

Torricelli, Robert, and Andrew Carroll. *In Our Own Words: Extraordinary Speeches of the American Century*. New York: Washington Square Press, 2000.

"Trip to Russia Topic of Samantha's Book." *News and Courier*. April 25, 1984.

U.S. Department of State. Unclassified. "Letter From Irina Tarnopol-sky to Andropov. June 1983." Case No. F-2011-25766 Doc. No. C05104822.

"U.S. Schoolgirl Who Toured U.S.S.R. Now Tours Japan." *Toledo Blade.* December 25, 1983.

Unger, Arthur. "Samantha Smith Takes Her Questions to Washington." *Christian Science Monitor.* January 16, 1984.

UPI. "From Russia Back to Regular Things." *New York Times.* July 23, 1983.

Venezia, Joyce A. "Samantha Smith Reacts to Jet Hit." *Beaver County Times.* September 7, 1983.

VideoSource, ABCNews. *Samantha Smith's Visit to the Russian Embassy.* YouTube. December 20, 1984. https://www.youtube.com/watch?v=5pv3inutuIg.

Volkova, Olga. "О Саманте, шоколадках, бантиках и бдительных спецслужбах. Саманта Смит в Артеке—как это было на самом деле (воспоминания ее вожатой) [On Samantha, choc-olates, bows, and vigilant intelligence agencies. Samantha Smith in Artek—how it actually happened (remembrances of her camp counselor)]." Artekovetc.ru. http://artekovetc.ru/samsmitvoj.html (accessed October 18, 2020).

Warner, Gale, and Michael Shuman. *Citizen Diplomats.* New York: Continuum, 1987.

Washburn, Karlene. "Arthur Smith a Guiding Light, Not Just for Sam." Unknown. 1985.

———. "Jane Smith Believes in 'Building a New Life.'" *Kennebec Journal.* June 19, 1986.

———. "Soviet Official to Attend Rites for Samantha." Guy Gannett Service. August, 1985.

Weible, Jack. "Samantha Takes a Breather before Meeting Media Again." *Kennebec Journal.* July 26, 1983.

———. "Samantha: There Is No Place like Home." *Kennebec Journal.* July 22, 1983.

"What They're Doing, Saying These Days." *Lewiston Daily Sun.* December 9, 1983.

Whittaker, Stephanie. "Nice Visit, but Samantha Says She'd Rather Live in Own Country." *Montreal Gazette*. July 22, 1983.

Wohlfert-Wihlborg, Lee, and Suzanne Adelson. "Famed as Andropov's Pen Pal, Samantha Smith Appears Again—as Robert Wagner's Co-star." *People*. June 3, 1985.

"Young Peace Ambassador, Father Die in Fiery Plane Crash." *Oklahoman*. August 27, 1985.

ABOUT THE AUTHOR

Lena Nelson is a writer, teacher, and citizen historian who has spent seventeen years researching and documenting the story of Samantha Smith and creating www.SamanthaSmith.info, the online archive of news articles and videos about Samantha Smith. She was a nominee for the Allegra Johnson Prize and has worked with numerous news, educational, and humanitarian organizations around the world. She has degrees in international studies and linguistics and lives with her family in Southern California.